WALKING IN THE
ISLES OF SCILLY

ABOUT THE AUTHOR

Paddy Dillon is a prolific outdoor writer with a score and more books to his name, as well as a dozen booklets and brochures. He writes for a number of outdoor magazines and other publications, as well as producing materials for tourism groups and other organisations. He lives on the fringe of the Lake District, and has walked, and written about walking, in every county in England, Scotland, Ireland and Wales. He generally leads at least one guided walking holiday overseas every year and has walked in many parts of Europe, as well as Nepal, Tibet and the Canadian Rockies.

While walking his routes, Paddy inputs his notes directly into a palm-top computer every few steps. His descriptions are therefore precise, having been written at the very point at which the reader uses them. He takes all his own photographs and often draws his own maps to illustrate his routes. He has appeared on television, and is a member of the Outdoor Writers' Guild.

WALKING IN THE
ISLES OF SCILLY

by

PADDY DILLON

CICERONE PRESS
MILNTHORPE, CUMBRIA, UK
www.cicerone.co.uk

© P. Dillon 2000
ISBN 1 85284 310 1
A catalogue record for this book is available from the British Library.

Advice to Readers

Readers are advised that while every effort is taken by the author to ensure the accuracy of this guidebook, changes can occur which may affect its contents. It is advisable to check locally on transport, accommodation, shops, etc, though even rights of way can be altered.

The publisher would welcome notes of any such changes.

Other Cicerone guide books by the same author
Irish Coastal Walks
The Irish Coast to Coast Walk
The Mountains of Ireland
Walking in Arran
Walking in County Durham
Walking in the Galloway Hills
Walking in the North Pennines
Channel Island Walks
GR20: Corsica – the High Level Route

Front cover: Walkers follow a path round one of the heathery headlands on the islands

CONTENTS

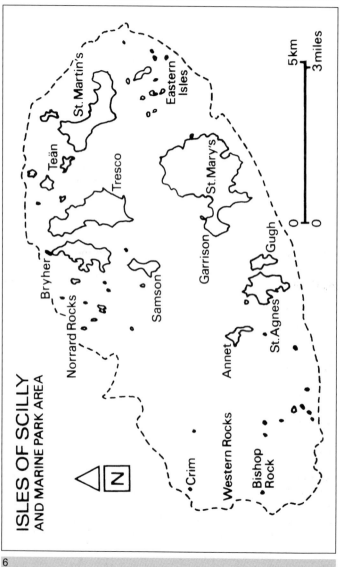

ISLES OF SCILLY
AND MARINE PARK AREA

N

St. Martin's

Eastern Isles

Teän

Tresco

St. Mary's

Bryher

Norrard Rocks

Samson

Garrison

Gugh

Annet

St. Agnes

Western Rocks

Crim

Bishop Rock

5 km
3 miles

INTRODUCTION

'Somewhere among the note-books of Gideon I once found a list of diseases as yet unclassified by medical science, and among these there occurred the word Islomania, which was described as a rare but by no means unknown affliction of spirit. There are people, Gideon used to say, by way of explanation, who find islands somehow irresistible. The mere knowledge that they are on an island, a little world surrounded by the sea, fills them with an indescribable intoxication.'

Lawrence Durrell, *Reflections on a Marine Venus*

Of all the British Isles, the Isles of Scilly are the most blessed. Basking in sunshine, rising green and pleasant from the blue Atlantic Ocean, fringed by rugged cliffs and sandy beaches, these self-contained little worlds are a joy to explore. There are no tall mountains, but the rocks around the coast are as dramatic as you'll find anywhere. There are no extensive moorlands, but you'll forget that as you walk round the open heathery headlands. The islands may be small in extent, but the eye is deceived and readily imagines vast panoramas and awesome seascapes. Views to the sea take in jagged rocks that have ripped many a keel and wrecked many a ship. The islands are clothed in colourful flowers, both cultivated and wild, and attract a rich bird life, including native breeding species and seasonal migrants.

The Isles of Scilly form the smallest of Britain's Areas of Outstanding Natural Beauty, and its historic shores have been designated as Heritage Coast. The surrounding sea is protected as a Marine Park. Archaeological remains abound, not only on the islands, but also submerged beneath the sea. The Isles of Scilly are special, revealing their secrets and charms to those who walk the headlands, sail from island to island, and take the time to observe the sights, sounds and scents of the landscape. While the walks in this guidebook could be completed in as little as a week, a fortnight would allow a much more leisurely appreciation of the islands, and leave you with memories that will last a lifetime.

LOCATION

The Isles of Scilly lie 28 miles (45km) west of Land's End: a position which ensures they are omitted from most maps of Britain, or shown only as insets. There are five inhabited islands and about fifty other areas that local people would call islands, as well as a hundred more rocks, and still more again at low water. The islands aren't part of Cornwall, but are a self-administering unit; you could think of this as the smallest 'county' in Britain. The total landmass is a mere 6¼ square miles (16 sq km). The waters around the Isles of Scilly, extending as far as the 165ft (50m) contour, form a Marine Park of around 50 square miles (125 sq km). Despite the small area of the islands, you can enjoy anything approaching 50 miles (80km) of truly remarkable walking in one of Britain's most charming and interesting landscapes.

GEOLOGY

The geology of the Isles of Scilly can be summed up in one word – granite. The islands are the south-western extremity of a deep-seated granite mass, or batholith, that reaches the surface of the earth around Dartmoor, Bodmin Moor and Land's End. Granite is the bedrock of the Isles of Scilly, and it breaks down to form a stony, sandy or gritty soil, as well as bright white sandy beaches. In some places around the coast and occasionally inland, the granite forms blocky cliffs and tors, rounded boulders or tilted slabs that have such a rough texture that they provide excellent grip for walkers. In other places chemical weathering of less stable minerals within the granite causes the rock to crumble, or peel away in layers. As a building material, granite has been used for centuries, but only in relatively recent times has it been possible to split the rock into squared blocks more suitable for substantial buildings.

While the Isles of Scilly escaped the Ice Age that affected much of Britain, it didn't escape the 'permafrost' conditions that pertained south of the ice sheets, breaking up the granite tors and forming a stony, sandy soil. Nor did the islands fare too well as the ice began to melt and sea levels began to rise. It's thought that Scilly became separated from the rest of Britain around 10,000 years ago. Scilly may well have been a single landmass for a while, but a combination of rising sea levels and coastal erosion produced the current pattern of five islands and a bewildering number of rocks and reefs. Before the arrival of the first settlers, it was no doubt a wild and wooded place.

ANCIENT HISTORY

Arthurian legend points to the Isles of Scilly as the last remnants of the lost land of Lyonesse; but while a submerged landscape does exist around the islands, it was never the Lyonesse of legend. In 1752 the Cornish antiquarian William Borlase discovered and recorded submerged field systems on the tidal flats near Samson. It seems that the first settlers were Neolithic, but a more comprehensive settlement of the islands came in the Bronze Age, up to 4000 years ago. Some splendid ritual standing stones and stoutly constructed burial chambers remain from this time, and excavations have revealed skeletons, cremated remains and a host of artefacts. When the Romans began their occupation of Britain 2000 years ago, criss-crossing the land with straight roads, settlement patterns on the Isles of Scilly were in huddled formations, as seen today on Halangy Down and Nornour. No doubt the Romans traded with the islands, as coins have been discovered, but it seems they established no lasting presence. In later centuries the Isles of Scilly attracted Christian hermits, leaving some of the islands blessed with the names of saints. That great seafaring race, the Vikings, also visited the islands. From time to time the Isles of Scilly have been a haven for pirates, and every now and then their haven was smashed by the authorities of the day. In the 11th century over one hundred pirates were beheaded in a single day on Tresco!

LATER HISTORY

A Benedictine priory was founded on Tresco in the 12th century, and Henry I granted the island to Tavistock Abbey. By the 14th century the islands were part of the Duchy of Cornwall and Edward III gave them to the Black Prince, who was made the Duke of Cornwall. In the 16th century Governor Francis Godolphin was granted the lease of the islands by Elizabeth I. Godolphin built the eight-pointed Star Castle above the harbour on St. Mary's. During the Civil War, in the middle of the 17th century, Prince Charles (later King Charles II) stayed briefly at the Star Castle. Towards the end of the Civil War the islands were occupied by disgruntled Royalists who launched pirate raids on passing ships, causing the Dutch to send a fleet of ships to deal with the problem. An English fleet intercepted the Dutch, preventing wholesale destruction on the islands, and gaining the final surrender of the Royalist force.

The 18th century was a time of great poverty on the islands, but despite their remoteness John Wesley visited them in the course of his preaching around the British Isles. Shipbuilding became an important occupation late in the 18th century and continued well into the 19th century. In the early 19th century the Godolphin family allowed their lease on the Isles of Scilly to lapse, so that they reverted to the Duchy of Cornwall. In 1834 Augustus Smith from Hertfordshire took over the lease of the islands as Lord Protector, and developed Tresco in particular, building the Abbey House as his residence and establishing the Abbey Gardens. The successful export of flowers from the islands dates from the middle of the 19th century and has enjoyed mixed fortunes. During 1918 the Dorrien-Smith family gave up the lease on all the islands except Tresco. While fortifications on St. Mary's were strengthened in the First World War, the islands escaped lightly from the conflict. During the Second World War, however, there was a lot more activity around the islands, as submarines and warships played deadly hide and seek manoeuvres in the waters, and several warplanes were stationed on the islands.

RECENT HISTORY

In a sudden magnanimous gesture in 1949, the Duchy of Cornwall offered the sale of the freehold on most properties occupied by sitting tenants in Hugh Town. The Isles of Scilly were designated as an Area of Outstanding Natural Beauty in 1975. The Duchy leased all its uninhabited islands and unfarmed wilderness land to the Isles of Scilly Environmental Trust in 1987. The Trust manages this land for conservation and recreation, safeguarding habitats for flora and fauna, while maintaining the network of footpaths over the land. The designation of a Marine Park to conserve the surrounding sea bed and marine life was another important development. The infrastructure of the islands continues to develop and tourism is an

Penzance harbour in Cornwall, from where the Scilonian III sets sail

increasingly important industry, but always with due regard to the environment and the conservation of nature.

These brief notes about the history of the Isles of Scilly give only the barest outline of some key events. The islands' history has been turbulent and colourful and makes an interesting and absorbing study. Be sure to visit the Isles of Scilly Museum in Hugh Town on St. Mary's for a more thorough grounding and to obtain further information.

GETTING TO THE ISLANDS

By Road and Rail: The rail network terminates at Penzance, with direct services from cities as distant as London, Birmingham and Glasgow. There are rail/sail deals available through the Isles of Scilly Travel Centre. A short walk from Penzance railway station, around the harbour, leads to the far quay where the *Scillonian III* sails for the Isles of Scilly. Cars cannot be taken over to the islands, but nor are they even necessary, so enquire about secure, long-term car parking around Penzance. If using a car to reach one of the airports listed below, again be sure to enquire about secure, long-term car parking arrangements. It's also possible to arrange transfers between Penzance railway station and Land's End airport, if you enquire while booking a flight.

By Ship: The *Scillonian III* is a fine little ship of 1000 tonnes, sailing once each way between Penzance and St. Mary's from Monday to Saturday throughout the year. In the high season there are usually two sailings on Saturdays, but only very rarely are there any sailings on Sundays. Observe the regulations for carrying luggage, which should always be labelled with your destination. Luggage can be conveyed to your accommodation in Hugh Town, but be sure to follow instructions to avail yourself of this service. The journey usually takes 2¾ hours. It's customary for the ship's whistle to sound half an hour before sailing to keep you on your toes! Bad weather can cause the schedule to be altered in the winter months. For details contact the Isles of Scilly Travel Centre on 0845-710555; Internet www.islesofscilly-travel.co.uk

By Aeroplane: Flights to St. Mary's are operated by Skybus, using Twin Otter or Islander aircraft. Flights from mainland airports are available from Land's End, Newquay, Exeter, Bristol and Plymouth. Flights are most frequent and shortest from Land's End, operating Monday to Saturday throughout the year and taking only fifteen minutes each way. Flights from the other airports are most frequent in the high season. For details contact the Isles of Scilly Travel Centre on 0845-710555; Internet www.islesofscilly-travel.co.uk

By Helicopter: Scotia Helicopter Services offer two services from Penzance using Sikorskys. Most flights are to St. Mary's, but some operate direct to Tresco, landing at a small heliport beside the Abbey Gardens. Flights operate Monday to Saturday throughout the year, with more during the high season. It's possible to enjoy some splendid aerial views of the islands using these services. On certain winter Saturdays it may not be possible to fly to Tresco. For details contact Scotia Helicopter Services on 01736-363871; or Internet www.helicopter-scilly.co.uk

GETTING AROUND THE ISLANDS

There is a bus service operating in a circuit around St. Mary's in the high season, as well as minibus and vintage bus tours around the island. There are also a handful of taxis, should you need to get to any place in a hurry. Most of the buses start from beside the little park near the Town Hall in the middle of Hugh Town, though you can always check what services are being offered at the Tourist Information Centre. There is an airport minibus service that operates from in front of the chemist's shop a short way inland from The Quay. The off-islands are small enough to walk around on foot

The launch collecting Samson's visitors from the sandy Bar Point

and you really don't need any other form of transport. If you choose an accommodation base on one of the off-islands, it might be possible for the proprietor to meet you at the quayside with a vehicle, but ask if this is possible when you book your accommodation.

St. Mary's Boatmen's Association operates eleven launches from Hugh Town on St. Mary's to the off-islands of St. Agnes, Bryher, Tresco and St. Martin's. Launches to Bryher may also stop at the uninhabited island of Samson on request. In addition, each of the off-islands has their own ferry services. Details of these services, plus a wealth of cruises, are advertised on noticeboards on The Quay at Hugh Town and at the quaysides on the off-islands, and can be obtained from the Tourist Information Centre. There is a small ticket kiosk run by St. Mary's Boatmen's Association on the Old Quay at Hugh Town. Remember that there will be more ferries and cruises to more places in the high season than in the winter months. Also bear in mind that the onset of stormy weather can lead to the sudden cancellation of all boat services around the islands. St. Mary's Boatmen's Association can be contacted at Rose Cottage, The Strand, St. Mary's, Isles of Scilly, TR21 0PT.

BOAT TRIPS

Quite apart from using boats as a means of access to islands and walks, you can also indulge yourself with a series of boat trips. Some trips are operated by the St. Mary's Boatmen's Association,

Boat trips and wildlife cruises around the islands are highly recommended

while others are run using small boats, which usually limit their passengers to twelve. Classic trips run by the St. Mary's Boatmen's Association include tours around the Western Rocks, Norrard Rocks, St. Helen's and Teän, the Eastern Isles, and a complete circuit around St. Mary's. There are 'Seabird Specials' for bird-watchers, historical tours, evening visits to St. Agnes for supper, and the chance to follow the popular 'gig races' in the high season. It's recommended that you sample some of these tours to broaden your experience of the islands, and you should make every effort to include as many of the remote islands and rocks as possible.

TOURIST INFORMATION

The Tourist Information Centre on St. Mary's can provide plenty of information about accommodation, pubs, restaurants, transport and attractions throughout the Isles of Scilly. Between April and October some 75,000 people stay on the islands, and an additional 25,000 people make day trips. In August the islands can run out of beds for visitors, so advance booking is always recommended. All the islands except Tresco have campsites. There are abundant self-catering cottages and chalets, as well as plenty of bed and breakfast establishments and guesthouses. There are ten hotels; six of them around Hugh Town on St. Mary's and one on each of the off-islands. For full details and a full colour brochure contact the Isles of Scilly Tourist Information Centre, Wesleyan Chapel, Well Lane, St.

Mary's, Isles of Scilly, TR21 0HZ. Telephone 01720-422536; Internet www.scillyonline.co.uk

MAPS OF THE ISLANDS

You could easily explore the Isles of Scilly without using maps, as the total land area is only 6¼ square miles (16 sq km), but you would miss a great deal along the way. Detailed maps will show you alternative routes and other options to the walks in this book. You'll also be able to identify dozens of near and distant features in view, as well as having all the relevant placenames at your fingertips. The following maps of the islands are available in a variety of scales and styles.

Ordnance Survey 1:25,000 Explorer 101 – Isles of Scilly. This gives the most accurate depiction of the Isles of Scilly on one large sheet, including all the rocks and reefs that make up the group, and a wealth of interesting and amazing placenames. The map also includes a small street plan of Hugh Town, and enlarged insets of southern Tresco and Penzance. Ordnance Survey grid references are used to indicate the starting point of each walk.

Ordnance Survey 1:50,000 Landranger 203 only shows the Isles of Scilly as an inset. The map gives insufficient detail of the islands and is not particularly recommended for walking or detailed exploring. It's a useful map if you are also considering walking around Land's End and The Lizard in Cornwall.

A Precious Heritage – visitors companion maps to the five inhabited islands, published by the Isles of Scilly Environmental Trust. These maps show virtually all roads, tracks and walkable paths. The unfarmed wilderness land managed by the Trust is distinguished from other tenanted land. A most useful series of maps, best used alongside the Ordnance Survey Explorer.

Free leaflets containing maps of all or some of the islands can be collected from the Tourist Information Centre or picked up from other locations. Some will prove useful, others less useful, and many of them exist to highlight a variety of services and attractions around the islands. Marine navigation charts are for those who sail as well as walk, or for serious marine studies.

The sketch maps in this guidebook show only the basic details of the islands and walking routes. A few of the maps aren't of walking routes, but show groups of islands that are covered by short descriptive chapters. There are also a few small-scale plans, showing greater detail of Hugh Town, The Garrison and Tresco Abbey Gardens.

THE WALKS

None of the walks on the Isles of Scilly could be described as difficult. The only way you could make them difficult is by rushing through them, which surely defeats the purpose of exploring the islands when there is so much of interest to see. The walks make use of a network of paths, mostly along the coast, but sometimes inland too. They may also follow tracks and roads, but the roads are likely to be free of traffic. Sensible precautions include wearing stout shoes or boots when walking along uneven or rocky paths, and carrying a set of waterproofs in case of rain. When stormy weather whips up the waves, you can get a drenching from salt spray, and it's always advisable to proceed with caution whenever walking close to breaking waves. There's always the chance that the next wave will break considerably higher. Unprotected cliffs also need to be approached cautiously, especially in high winds or blustery conditions. The sun can be exceptionally strong, so if you burn easily then be sure to keep your skin covered, either with light-coloured, lightweight, comfortable polycotton clothing or a high-factor sunscreen. A good sunhat is also useful; one that ties on so that it won't be blown away and lost at sea!

The walks included in this guidebook will allow you to explore the coastlines of the five inhabited islands, as well as some of the smaller islands. With the aid of cruises you can enjoy close-up views of the Eastern Isles, Norrard Rocks, Western Rocks and even the solitary pillar of the Bishop Rock Lighthouse. It all depends how long you are staying on the islands and how much you wish to see. If you were in a hurry you could just about complete all these walks in a week, but two weeks would give a more leisurely chance to explore. Better still, make two or three trips throughout the year to appreciate the changing seasons. By no means do the walks in this book exhaust all the possibilities for exploring the islands, and there are just as many paths left for you to discover for yourself. Apart from the walking route descriptions, there are also short descriptions of groups of small islands that you might well choose to visit, but where the walking potential is really quite limited.

GUIDED WALKS

You can enhance your visit to the Isles of Scilly by taking part in a series of guided walks that are available in the high season. There are walks led by knowledgeable local people, with a specific emphasis on wildlife and heritage. By joining one of these walks you have a chance to keep up to date with what is happening in the natural world. Flowers bloom and fade, birds come and go on their migrations, and a good guide will be able to explain what is currently happening around the islands. Furthermore, you have the chance to ask specific questions on the spot. For details of guided walks, enquire at the Tourist Information Office or the Isles of Scilly Environmental Trust Office. There are also specific wildlife cruises – some operating during the day and others departing at dusk, depending on what is to be sighted.

Island Wildlife Tours offers visitors the chance to discover the rich variety of wildlife around the Isles of Scilly in the company of a resident naturalist and ornithologist. For full details of the tours contact: Will Wagstaff, 42 Sallyport, St. Mary's, Isles of Scilly, TR21 0JE. Telephone 01720-422212; Email <u>william.</u> <u>wagstaff@virgin.net</u>

ISLAND FLOWERS

There are two broad classes of flowers on the Isles of Scilly: those grown for sale and shipment to the mainland, and those that grow in the wild. Bear in mind that wild flowers do creep into the culti-vated flower fields, and some of the cultivated flowers have a habit of hopping out into the wilds! The flower industry started in 1868 when the tenant of Rocky Hill Farm on St. Mary's packed some flowers into a box and sent them to Covent Garden. Within a few years there were fields of daffodils and narcissus being grown. Visitors expecting to see fields of golden blooms will be disap-pointed, as the flowers are cut before they bloom. A field of wonderful blooms is technically a failed crop! To protect the tiny flower fields from wind and salt spray, tall, dense windbreak hedgerows are planted. Hedging species include pittosporum, euonymus and veronica, though there are also tall shelter belts of long-established Monterey and lodgepole pines. There are flower farms on each of the inhabited islands, and some specialise in posting fresh flowers to British destinations on request. There are also bulb farms, from which you can take away a selection of bulbs that are more likely to survive the journey home in your own care.

Wild flowers number around 700 species around the Isles of Scilly, making any attempt to list them here a rather pointless exercise. There are some plants that are peculiar to the islands, either growing nowhere else in Britain or being sub-species of plants that do grow in Britain. Almost 250 species are included on the Isles of Scilly Environmental Trust Flower Checklist, which is an invaluable leaflet to carry around the islands, along with a good field guide to flowering plants. Common plants include bracken, heather and gorse on most open uncultivated areas, with bulbous cushions of thrift on many cliffs and rocky areas. Perhaps one of the most startling escapees from the flower fields are large agapanthus blooms, which now decorate many sand dunes, growing among the marram grass. Fleshy Hottentot figs also creep through the dunes. The Tresco Abbey Gardens contain 3000 species, making that one small area a very special place for more careful study.

ISLAND BIRDS

The Isles of Scilly are renowned for their bird life, and while resident breeding species may be few in number, the islands are an important landfall for many more migrant species in the spring and autumn. Up to 400 species of birds have been recorded around the islands, but this includes some extremely uncommon birds that somehow find themselves well off their usual migratory routes. Almost 150 species are included on the Isles of Scilly Environmental Trust Bird Checklist, which is an invaluable leaflet to carry around the islands, along with a good field guide to birds.

Seabirds are, of course, plentiful. Herring gulls, greater and lesser black-backed gulls and kittiwakes are fairly common. Four species of terns are also present, including Arctic terns on their round-the-world migrations. Cormorants and shags often frequent isolated rocks and cliff ledges, easily spotted because of their habit of holding their wings outstretched for long periods. By taking a wildlife cruise you can see great 'rafts' of shags far out to sea, and maybe also smaller 'rafts' of Manx shearwaters.

Auks include guillemots and razorbills, sleeker and more slender than the comical puffins which are eagerly awaited each spring by bird-watchers. During the breeding season male puffins

Gulls are everywhere, but the islands boast plenty of rare birds too

have rainbow-hued bills, used for courtship display, aggression against other males, and for digging burrows. Like the Manx shearwater, puffins nesting on dry land live in mortal fear of gulls. Storm petrels and fulmar petrels nest in isolated places, out on remote rocky ledges or on the island sanctuary of Annet. With their amazing flying dives, gannets provide the most startling feeding display of any of the seabirds. While it's normal for people to imagine them spearing fish with their bills, they actually seem to catch fish while swimming back to the surface. The intertidal flats, especially around the shallow lagoon in the middle of the Isles of Scilly, attract a host of waders. Piping oystercatchers probe the sands, while turnstones, naturally, prefer to turn over stones in search of food. Sanderlings, sand pipers, whimbrel and ringed plovers may also be seen on the sands, with rock pipits preferring the higher, drier regions of the beaches. 'Seabird 2000' was a comprehensive count of all seabird species around Britain that took place during the years 1999–2001. Counting the birds around the Isles of Scilly involved volunteers having to visit most of the exposed rocks around the islands.

While there are no great freshwater lakes on the Isles of Scilly, there are several small pools and ponds. Many of these attract waterfowl and some have been equipped with bird hides to aid observation. A few uncommon species of herons have been spotted around the islands. Snipe, redshanks and greenshanks are attracted to water, along with moorhens, ducks, geese and swans. Water rails are commonly spotted, and it's worth looking out for little egrets in the autumn. As many of the pools are surrounded by reeds and willows, a variety of warblers, wagtails and flycatchers find them a favourable habitat. Kingfishers, though extremely uncommon, often startle birdwatchers with a sudden flash of iridescent colour.

There are plenty of birds to be spotted around the fields and hedgerows. Wrens, though tiny, are really quite numerous. Blackbirds and thrushes, swallows and martins, finches and tits all favour these habitats, while more open spaces may feature redwing and fieldfare. Stonechats have a preference for gorse bushes. Cuckoos are often heard earlier in the Isles of Scilly than mainland Britain, and the poor rock pipits often find themselves raising cuckoo chicks. Birds of prey include kestrels, merlins, peregrines and hobbies. Birds that you shouldn't expect to see include owls, magpies and woodpeckers, but occasionally a true rarity blows in from distant climes.

ISLAND ANIMALS

Apart from domestic farm stock and pets, you'll see very few animals on the Isles of Scilly. A few rabbits maybe, but little else, unless you're lucky enough to spot some of the few bats that hunt insects at dusk. One peculiar little creature is the Scilly shrew, which is a distinct variation from its mainland cousins. Introduced animals include hedgehogs, which are present on St. Mary's, and slow worms on Bryher. Looking to the sea, however, there are a surprising number of large mammals. Grey seals can be observed resting on remote shores and tidal ledges. Dolphins and porpoises are occasionally spotted around the islands, but more often favour the open ocean, as do more rarely spotted pilot and killer whales.

Although the waters around the Isles of Scilly are protected as a Marine Park, few visitors are aware of the importance of this habitat. Four special areas within the Marine Park have been identified. The Western Rocks are described as 'super-exposed' and can support only the hardiest communities of plants and animals. St. Agnes and Annet have pebbly seabeds around them, supporting a range of rare seaweeds. The east coast of St. Mary's has sheltered bedrock providing a habitat for solitary corals, branched sponges, delicate sea fans and other species. The flats around Samson, Tresco and St. Martin's are the shallowest waters around the Isles of Scilly, with rich communities of seaweeds and animals. An abundance of hard-shelled molluscs include scallops, limpets, razor shells, cowries and periwinkles. Sea urchins are numerous, but live in deep water and only occasionally are their shells cast ashore. Crabs and lobsters are still lifted in traditional pots.

Fishing is a minor occupation on the Isles of Scilly, but it's interesting to see what species are caught in the surrounding waters. Dogfish and rays are present, and their egg cases can be found on the shores. Plaice, sole, skate, mackerel, cod, monkfish, pollock, turbot, mullet and hake are all caught. There are conger eels and squid, and every so often peculiar species such as marlin and sea horses make their way into these waters. Commercial shrimping and prawning is restricted to three months in the summer. Very occasionally huge basking sharks are seen, their enormous mouths filtering the water for the tiniest marine organisms. These sharks used to be hunted for the oil in their livers, but nowadays are something of a rarity. Most of the fish caught commercially are packed away to the mainland, but local fishermen also supply some of the hotels, guesthouses and restaurants with freshly caught fish.

ISLES OF SCILLY ENVIRONMENTAL TRUST

The Trust was formed in 1985, and by 1987 had secured a 99-year lease on all the unfarmed wilderness land owned by the Duchy of Cornwall. This includes substantial areas of St. Mary's, St. Agnes and Gugh, Bryher and St. Martin's, as well as all the uninhabited islands and rocks. Tresco, which is leased to Robert Dorrien-Smith, is not managed by the Trust. The remit of the Trust is wide-ranging, but basically encompasses maintaining a balance between wildlife conservation and recreation. Trust staff maintain the footpath network on the islands, and have an ongoing programme to control bracken and gorse and to replenish the native tree cover. You can help by contributing to a tree-planting scheme. Ancient monuments need to be cleared of scrub and protected from damage, important nesting sites for birds need to be kept free from interference, and constant monitoring of the environment is necessary. It all takes time and it costs money. Visitors to the Isles of Scilly are invited to become 'Friends of Scilly' by contributing to the work of the Trust. It's also worth visiting the Trust office in Hugh Town, where a wealth of interesting publications can be purchased. Trust staff also occasionally lead walks and wildlife trips. Contact the Isles of Scilly Environmental Trust, Carn Thomas, Hugh Town, St. Mary's, Isles of Scilly, TR21 0PT. Telephone 01720-422153.

THE DUCHY OF CORNWALL

Many visitors to the Isles of Scilly wonder about the role of the Duchy of Cornwall, since mention is made of this body virtually everywhere. The Duchy is a series of estates, by no means all in Cornwall, but throughout Britain, which exist to provide an income to the heir to the throne. Established in the 14th century, the extent of land controlled by the Duchy has varied, but has always included the Isles of Scilly. As the islands' landlord, the Duchy has always raised its revenue through the sale of leases and collection of rents on the land. Some of the earliest rents were paid in the form of salted puffins! It is probably through the influence of Prince Charles that the Duchy has an increased awareness of the environmental and aesthetic value of the land in its control. There are information boards in the harbour waiting room on St. Mary's that outline the role of the Duchy in the life of the islands. The Duchy office is at Hugh House on the Garrison above Hugh Town on St. Mary's.

PLAN OF THIS GUIDE

The plan of this guidebook is simple. The first few walks are on St. Mary's, taking in a town trail around Hugh Town, a stroll around The Garrison, then more extended walks around the coast and nature trails of St. Mary's. The rest of the islands are visited in a roughly clockwise direction, with Gugh and St. Agnes being explored in turn. There are short chapters on some of the smaller islands and groups of islets and rocks – as visits must be by boat trip, no walking routes are offered. Thus, the guidebook works its way around Annet and the Western Rocks, Samson, Bryher and the Norrard Rocks. Tresco and the little islands of St. Helen's and Teän give way to St. Martin's and the Eastern Isles, bringing this delightful tour around the Isles of Scilly full circle.

WALK 1:

HUGH TOWN TRAIL

The main settlement on St. Mary's used to be Old Town, but during the construction of the defences around the Garrison, people drifted onto the narrow neck of land between the harbour and Porth Cressa, and Hugh Town grew throughout the 17th century. Hugh Town is by far the largest settlement on the Isles of Scilly. In a sense, it is the islands' capital, but it has the appearance of a small town or large village.

A stroll around Hugh Town is something you should complete at the start of your exploration of the Isles of Scilly, so that you're aware of the islands' greatest range of services, and you know where to find things and how the place operates. Hugh Town, for all its small size, is packed with history and heritage, and all kinds of interesting corners. Most buildings are built of granite, the bedrock of the islands, and they stand cheek by jowl on a narrow neck of land between the Garrison and the larger part of St. Mary's. Take special note of all the slide shows that are offered in the evenings in the high season. These are presented by knowledgeable local people with a passion for the history, heritage, flowers and wildlife of the islands.

The route

Distance: 1½ miles (2.5km)
Start: Harbourside Hotel on The Quay, 902109

The Quay is an obvious place to start this walk. Those who reach the Isles of Scilly using the *Scillonian III* place their feet on this stout granite quay before walking anywhere else in the islands. The Quay connects Rat Island to Hugh Town, with the oldest parts closest to town, dating from 1603, but don't rush straight into town. The Harbourside Hotel sits on Rat Island, offering food and drink right at the start. The ferry waiting room beside the hotel is full of inform-

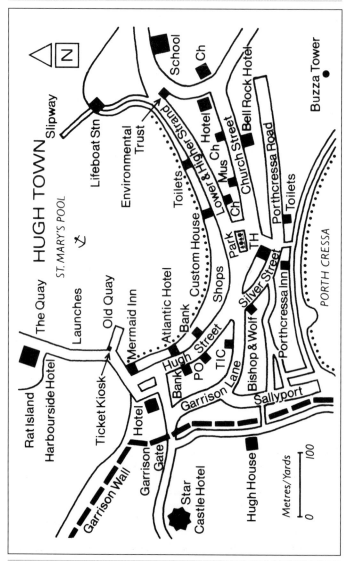

ative panels about the history and natural history of the islands, and these are well worth a few minutes of study. Some panels also offer information about the Duchy of Cornwall.

When you follow The Quay towards town, take note of all the noticeboards advertising ferries to the off-islands, wildlife cruises, evening cruises and all the rest. There is a small stone kiosk on the Old Quay where you can obtain tickets for the off-islands launches and cruises run by St. Mary's Boatmen's Association. For most other cruises and trips, you either book in advance or pay on board. Ten o'clock in the mornings is the busiest time in high season, when everyone flocks down to the quays for their tickets and the launches take their first eager passengers to all the off-islands.

Turn left at the Mermaid Inn and walk along Hugh Street. The Pilot's Gig Restaurant if off to the right, but you continue straight onwards, passing the Atlantic Hotel, which is on the left. Hugh Street is like a canyon of granite and it's fortunate that so few vehicles use it, as space is limited. The Post Office stands beside a rugged granite arch and bears a stone marked 'VR 1897'. A fine granite terrace of houses continues on that side of the street, while the Isles of Scilly Steamship Company office is on the left. A group of gift shops are clustered around a road junction. The Bishop & Wolf is a bar and restaurant to the right, but you should keep left to reach a more open square. The Town Hall stands to the right, carrying a datestone of 1897, and the small green space in the middle of Hugh Town serves as the town park. Taxis, small tour buses and splendid vintage buses may be parked here, if you fancy a quick spin around St. Mary's along its rather limited road network.

Keep left of the little park, following Lower Strand Street, passing Armorel Cottage and its huge cactus plant. The Custom House is to the left, and the Star of the Sea Catholic Church is to the right. A toilet block stands beside a short promenade path, where there are fine views across the harbour, while inland, shops give way to a terrace of houses. The Lifeboat Station is tucked under a granite tor and is served by a short path. If you follow it, then you have to return afterwards. The newest lifeboat is called *The White-heads* and is too big for the station, so you'll see it moored out on the harbour instead.

The road called Higher Strand climbs uphill, but you should

Armorel Cottage and its giant cactus near the little park in Hugh Town

turn sharply right at the top to discover the Isles of Scilly Environmental Trust office. When this is open you can obtain a wealth of literature about the flora and fauna of the islands. The staff are very helpful if you have any particular questions or interests. They may have a series of wildlife walks or cruises planned, if you wish to take part. Just around the corner is the Parish Church of St. Mary the Virgin, dating from 1835, and you'll also see a cylindrical granite tower on Buzza Hill, which was once a windmill. Walk straight down into town along Church Street. The Hotel Godolphin is on the right, as well as the Methodist Church. There may be a notice posted at the church detailing evening slide shows. The Bell Rock Hotel is on the left.

The Isles of Scilly Museum stands on the right, in a rather faceless modern building. Don't be put off by the façade, as the interior is absolutely packed with interest. You'll find plenty of items relating to the history and heritage of the islands, as well as exhibits detailing the flora and fauna. It's usual for some of the flowers and shrubs that grow around the Isles of Scilly to be arranged in jars or pots, changed every few days, so that you can be absolutely sure about identifying the wealth of species you'll spot outdoors. When you leave the museum, the Church Hall is also on the right, and again there may be a notice posted detailing evening slide shows. A terrace of granite guesthouses leads back to the little park and the Town Hall.

Turn left and climb up a few steps on an embankment to see Porth Cressa Beach. There is a toilet block to the left and the Porthcressa Inn is to the right. Walk back down the steps and turn left along Silver Street, behind the Town Hall, and head back into the middle of Hugh Town. Turn left at Mumford's, where you can buy books, maps, postcards and the like. To the right is the Tourist Information Centre in the Old Wesleyan Chapel. You can obtain all the information you need about accommodation options, as well as checking opening times of attractions around the islands.

Follow Garrison Lane uphill. The police station is on the right, but you turn left along Sallyport. Look for a sign above a passageway marked 'Garrison Through Archway' and you'll be led through a terrace of houses and under the Garrison Walls by way of the low-roofed Sallyport. You emerge onto a narrow road near Hugh House, which is the Duchy of Cornwall office. Turn left to reach the Garden Battery, where you can enjoy a view over the rooftops of Hugh Town and appreciate just how compact the little town really is. Follow the road past the Higher Battery, then turn left uphill. You can visit the Powder Magazine Exhibition and learn about the fortifications of the Garrison, or continue up to the Star Castle Hotel. When you walk back downhill afterwards, you pass through an old archway dated 1742 at Gatehouse Cottage. Walk downhill past Tregarthen's Hotel, which was founded by Captain Tregarthen. He used to bring passengers to the Isles of Scilly 150 years ago, whenever he brought supplies from the mainland. There was a catch; his guests couldn't leave the islands until he went back to the mainland for more supplies! Turn left below the hotel to return to the harbour where the town trail started.

Facilities in Hugh Town

- There are six **hotels** around Hugh Town and the largest concentration of **guest houses** and **bed and breakfast** establishments in the Isles of Scilly, as well as **abundant self-catering accommodation**.
- The only two **banks** in the Isles of Scilly, Barclays and Lloyds, the latter with an ATM, are in Hugh Town.
- There is a **Post Office**, **chemist** and **newsagent**, as well as several **shops** selling provisions and souvenirs.

- There are several **pubs** and **restaurants**, and in the high season it's wise to book a table in advance for meals.

- The **museum**, **police station**, **hospital**, and indeed all administrative services for the islands are in Hugh Town.

- As the hub of activity in the islands, all **ferries** use the harbour, while tour **buses** and **taxis** serve St. Mary's from the centre of Hugh Town.

- **Churches** include St. Mary the Virgin (Church of England), Our Lady Star of the Sea Catholic Church and the Methodist Church. Toilets are located on The Quay, on The Strand and at Porth Cressa.

Basically, if you can't find what you need in Hugh Town, you probably won't find it on the islands!

WALK 2:

THE GARRISON WALL

The promontory to the west of Hugh Town is almost completely encircled by a stout defensive wall bristling with batteries. The Garrison was developed in stages over three centuries, but the most significant starting date is 1593, when Governor Francis Godolphin built the eight-pointed Star Castle. Additional walls and batteries were built around the promontory, with more appearing during the Civil War. The Garrison held out as a Royalist stronghold until 1651. Other islands holding out to the bitter end included Jersey, in the Channel Islands, and Inishbofin, off the west coast of Ireland. The Garrison came to resemble its present form during restructuring associated with the Wars of the Spanish Succession and the Napoleonic Wars. During the two world wars, there were few alterations, except for the positioning of pillboxes into some of the batteries. Even while it was manned by soldiers, the Garrison Wall provided a leisurely walk for 18th- and 19th-century visitors, and it still does so admirably today. English Heritage produces an excellent leaflet map and guide to the Garrison, and a visit to the Powder Magazine Exhibition is highly recommended.

Accommodation is available within the Garrison Wall at two remarkably different locations. The Star Castle Hotel is one of the more exclusive hotels in the Isles of Scilly, offering some rooms with four-poster beds in keeping with the history of the place. The hotel also has a Dungeon Bar! High on the headland is the Garrison Farm campsite, the only campsite on St. Mary's, and one of only four campsites around the Isles of Scilly.

The route

Distance: 1½ *miles (2.5km)*
Start: *Garrison Gate in Hugh Town, 901106*

A steep, stone-paved road runs up from Hugh Town to the Garrison

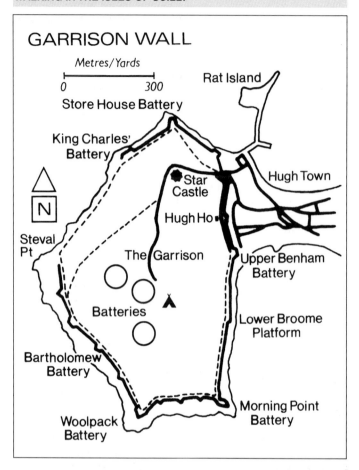

Gate. You can see the date 1742 carved in stone above the moulded archway, below a little bellcote. The Guardhouse and Gatehouse Cottage stand just inside the archway. You can visit the Powder Magazine Exhibition straight ahead, if you want to make an in-depth study of the fortifications, otherwise turn left to start walking clockwise around the walls. A narrow road rises to the Higher

Battery, where you can look over the rooftops of Hugh Town. Walk to the Garden Battery, which is in front of Hugh House, the Duchy of Cornwall office. A little further along, the road passes over a sallyport: a narrow, low-roofed passageway beneath the wall. It's worth taking a peek under the wall at this point, but mind your head if you are tall. The next battery is the Upper Benham Battery, which overlooks Porth Cressa Beach.

Continue along a stony track parallel to the Garrison Wall, passing the Upper Broome Platform. Trees flank the track as it passes the Lower Broome Platform. At this point the wall takes a slight step back from the cliffs, and you can distinguish the line of an older breastwork along the cliff-top. The Morning Point Battery occupies a rocky promontory with sweeping views, and its cannons had clear lines of fire to the north, east, south and west. As you walk around the southern portion of the Garrison Wall, the wall is again a step back from the cliff and the line of a former breastwork can be distinguished.

The Woolpack Battery stands on another rocky promontory offering a good range for cannon fire. Two big cannons here were salvaged from a wreck. Views across St. Mary's Sound take in Gugh, St. Agnes, Annet and the Bishop Rock Lighthouse. Walk to Bartholomew Battery and up past Colonel George Boscawen's Battery. You'll notice a peculiar structure partly buried underground, and this was an engine room that generated power for a series of range-finding searchlights in the early 20th century.

Further along the track there is a fork, and you could go either way. If you follow the track uphill to the right, then you'll be led quickly and easily past some wind-blasted pines to reach the Star Castle. If you follow the line of the Garrison Wall, however, you'll find it ends quite suddenly below the Steval Point Battery. You can bear right and continue along the cliffs, looking at the breastwork and batteries that preceeded the Garrison Wall, dating from the Civil War period. The course of the wall resumes at the King Charles' Battery, and can be followed to the Store House Battery in front of Newman House.

Although the Garrison Wall continues along the cliffs from Newman House to Hugh Town, you will actually have to leave it and walk uphill to return to the Garrison Gate. If you wish to visit the eight-pointed Star Castle, then turn sharply right just before

A granite archway gives access to the Woolpack Battery on the Garrison

reaching the Garrison Gate and follow the road uphill. The castle has been a hotel since the 1930s and is one of the most unusual places you could choose as an accommodation base in the Isles of Scilly. There are further explorations you could make on the high ground within the Garrison. There is a campsite and access to an early 20th-century hilltop battery. When your wanderings are completed, simply walk back through the Garrison Gate to return to Hugh Town.

Facilities on the Garrison

The Garrison is immediately alongside Hugh Town, so all the facilities of the town are readily available as detailed in the Hugh Town trail.

• Within the Garrison Wall are the **Star Castle Hotel** and the **Garrison Farm campsite**.

The little island of Gweal and some of the jagged Norrard Rocks

The remains of a 12th-century priory at the Abbey Gardens on Tresco

Innisidgen Upper Burial Chamber on St. Mary's is 4000 years old

Walker perched on a granite outcrop on Shipman Head Down on Bryher

The Isles have a colourful
and turbulent history

Seals can be approached
quite closely on boat trips

The exotic Tresco Abbey Gardens
were founded by Augustus Smith

The Nag's Head, a natural
sculpture of a horse's head

WALK 3:

ST. MARY'S COAST

The longest coastal walk you can follow in the Isles of Scilly is around St. Mary's. It will take you most of the day to complete. It's not particularly difficult, but there are a lot of ups and downs, and ins and outs along the way. There are also plenty of interesting things to see: notably old fortifications, a host of ancient burial cairns and a well-preserved ancient village site. If you find yourself running out of time, you could detour inland onto the roads and hope to intercept the bus service, but carry the current bus timetable if you plan to do this.

The scenery around the coast varies tremendously, taking in cosy little coves, awesome granite headlands, areas of woodland and open heath, and always, always the surging sea. With a favourable tide you could include a short detour onto Toll's Island, which is connected to St. Mary's by a sandy bar. The route crosses part of the little airport, where you must obey the pedestrian traffic lights and sirens when aircraft are landing or taking off. When you reach Old Town, you could cut the walk short and head back along the road to Hugh Town, on foot or by bus, saving the rugged Peninnis Head for another day.

If you are feeling fit and still have a little energy to spare on your return to Hugh Town, then by all means complete a lap around the Garrison Wall, as outlined in Walk 2. The addition of the Garrison Wall walk will ensure that you really do walk the entire coastline of St. Mary's.

The route

Distance: 10 miles (16km)
Start: Town Hall in Hugh Town, 903105

If you are based in Hugh Town, then the Town Hall makes a good reference point for the start of this walk. Face the little park and

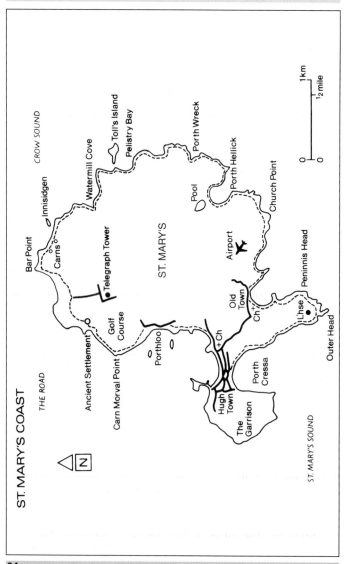

ST. MARY'S COAST

N

THE ROAD

CROW SOUND

Bar Point
Innisidgen
Carns
Watermill Cove
Toll's Island
Pelistry Bay
Porth Wreck
Porth Hellick
Church Point
Pool
Telegraph Tower
ST. MARY'S
Airport
Ancient Settlement
Golf Course
Carn Morval Point
Porthloo
Old Town
Ch
Ch
Peninnis Head
L'hse
Outer Head
Hugh Town
The Garrison
Porth Cressa
ST. MARY'S SOUND

1km
½ mile
0
0

keep to the left of it, following Lower Strand Street and passing Armorel Cottage with its huge cactus plant. There's a short promenade path beside the road, with fine views over the harbour. The Lifeboat Station is tucked under a granite tor and is served by a short path. If you follow it, then return afterwards and walk up the road called Higher Strand, passing the secondary school and continuing downhill. Turn left as signposted for Harry's Walls, and you can follow other signs to make a short detour uphill to see the remains of this unfinished 16th-century fort. The track along the shore passes craft workshops and joins a road. Turn left to follow the road uphill, overlooking Newford Island and enjoying widening views across the harbour.

Turn left along a path to pass Juliet's Garden Restaurant above Porthloo, with its delightfully flowery terrace. Three gates lead through fields to reach an open slope above the sea. Bracken and brambles flank the path as it approaches Carn Morval Point, then the path cuts across a heathery slope. There are views of Annet, Samson, Bryher, Tresco, St. Helen's, Round Island, Teän and St. Martin's. You may also notice that there's a nine-hole golf course above you. Follow the path down through bracken, until diverted inland and uphill on Halangy Down. Here you can inspect the remains of an ancient village site, admiring the interlinked round houses and the little paths between them. The site is around 2000 years old. On the brow of Halangy Down is Bant's Carn burial chamber – a much older structure dating back some 4000 years.

Head for some tall masts on the brow of Halangy Down and go through a gate. Turn right to walk uphill. (Bear in mind that you could continue inland by road to the Telegraph Tower if you wanted to catch a bus back to Hugh Town.) Watch for a sign on the left pointing along a track to show the way to the Innisidgen burial chambers. Follow this track along, then left and downhill. When it reaches the shore, continue along a path through marram grass and bracken. The Innisidgen Lower Chamber is perched on a grassy bank to the right, then you follow a path up a slope of bracken to reach the Innisidgen Upper Chamber. This is a more impressive structure, with views out to St. Martin's and the Eastern Isles, and tall, dark Monterey pines on the slope above.

Follow the path further around the coast, across another slope of bracken, to reach Block House Point. There are the scanty remains of an old block house and breastwork defences on the slope. The path moves inland around a little valley above Watermill Cove. Stay high on another series of paths through more bracken then descend to a sandy beach overlooking Toll's Island. A sand bar links the little island to St. Mary's at low tide, so you may be able to include it in the circuit. A path leads to Pelistry Bay and around a couple more rugged headlands, where intriguing rocky tors are passed on the way to Porth Wreck. It's worth climbing straight uphill from this rugged little cove to see a burial chamber on top of Porth Hellick Down. This is the largest of eight burial cairns – the other seven being difficult to locate on the ground sloping towards Porth Hellick. Curiously, views from the mound extend across most of St. Mary's, but none of the other islands are seen. There are some huge boulders of granite on the heathery down, as well as rocky points extending into the sea, and towering tors around Porth Hellick. One of the most prominent tors is known as the Loaded Camel.

As you walk round the shingly embankment at the head of Porth Hellick, you pass a memorial stone to Sir Cloudesley Shovell, a Rear-Admiral in the Navy until his death nearby in 1707. A fleet of twenty-one ships was sailing to Portsmouth on 22nd October 1707 and would have made it safely past the Isles of Scilly if the Rear-Admiral hadn't ordered the fleet to heave-to and take soundings. Four ships, including the Rear-Admiral's flagship *Association*, were wrecked on the Western Rocks. Although the Rear-Admiral escaped in a barge, along with his greyhound and a large treasure chest, he suffered another wrecking while making for St. Mary's, and his body was brought ashore and buried at Porth Hellick. It was later removed to Westminster Abbey for reburial. Some 1670 sailors were drowned that night, and the incident remains one of the worst out of almost a thousand wreckings around the islands. The exact site where the *Association* sank was not discovered until 1967.

There is access to the Higher Moors nature trail from Porth Hellick, and you can refer to Walk 4 for more details. Continue around the next rugged headland on Salakee Down, through bracken and over heathery slopes, enjoying the rocky coast below. Watch out for aircraft at the end of the airport runway, observing the warning signs and pedestrian traffic lights. This is no place to

The little lighthouse on Penninis Head near Old Town on St. Mary's

loiter or stop for a picnic! The path continues towards the little village of Old Town, passing the rocky Tolman Point on the way. You could take a break at the Old Town Café at a road junction. Old Town used to be the main settlement on St. Mary's, with Castle Ennor as the main defence. The castle site is now lacking any stonework and Old Town is a mere village, since people drifted to Hugh Town in the 17th century. If you've had enough for one day, you can save the walk around Peninnis Head for another day, and either walk back along the road to Hugh Town or catch one of the airport shuttle buses, or the bus service that runs all around the island, to return to town.

To continue with the walk, turn left along the road at the head of Old Town Bay, then left again to pass the Old Church. Labour party members may wish to pay their respects to a past Prime Minister, Harold Wilson, who is buried in the churchyard and who had a great affection for the Isles of Scilly. The path is flanked by tall hedges as it passes a couple of fields, then it passes the spiky tor of Carn Leh. Continue along the path, staying just above the rocky coast rather than climbing higher on Peninnis Head. There are huge blocky outcrops, towering tors, precariously perched boulders, great flat slabs and areas of strangely fluted water-worn granite. Pulpit Rock and the Outer Head are places of bizarre rock-forms well worth a few moments of careful study. Pass below the little Peninnis Lighthouse and take in a view of Gugh, St. Agnes and Annet across St. Mary's Sound. As you walk further round the headland you can see the Garrison Wall and Bryher. The path leads

Pulpit Rock is one of the more bizarre rock formations on Peninnis Head

around the coast, diverting uphill and inland to avoid an eroded stretch of coast, then it runs down to the beach at Porth Cressa.

You can call a halt to the walk here, and the Town Hall is just a step inland. There are abundant offers of food and drink at various pubs and restaurants, the nearest being the Porthcressa Inn. If you feel you could go on and complete the walk around the Garrison Wall too, then refer to the route description in Walk 2 and enjoy the rest of the coast of St. Mary's.

Facilities around St. Mary's coast

Hugh Town, at the start and finish of the walk, has the greatest range of services on the route.

- The walk itself passes **craft shops** on the way out of town, as well as Juliet's Garden Restaurant above Porthloo.

- The only other places offering **food and drink** are towards the end of the walk – the Old Town Café and Lock Stock & Barrel at Old Town.

- **Accommodation** is similarly sparse around the coast, though there are a couple of guesthouses and a few self-catering cottages and chalets a short distance inland.

- There's also a **bus** service that makes a circuit of the island's roads, which could be used to split the route at Telegraph or Old Town.

WALK 4:

ST. MARY'S NATURE TRAILS

If you think that all the walking on the Isles of Scilly must be within sight of the sea, then this walk challenges that view. There are two nature trails on St. Mary's: the Higher Moors and the Lower Moors. These nature trails are for the most part enclosed by patchy woodlands, hedgerows or reed beds. Views from them tend to be of nearby farmland, and only at a couple of corners do they run close enough to the sea for you to be able to see it. Starting from the little village of Old Town, only a short walk from Hugh Town, you can enjoy the Lower Moors nature trail first. Farm tracks and quiet roads can be used to reach the Telegraph Tower, which is the highest point on the Isles of Scilly, then link with the Higher Moors nature trail. This leads you almost to the sea at Porth Hellick, but there are leafy paths and tracks climbing up to the airport, from where roads lead you back to Old Town.

The route

> Distance: 5 miles (8km)
> Start: Old Town Café, 914102

The Old Town Café stands at a crossroads in the little village of Old Town. Walk inland along a quiet little road with a rough surface. After passing only a few houses, a gate gives access to the Lower Moors nature trail. As you follow a path between bushes and reed beds, there are two bird hides off to the left overlooking a small reedy pool. There is also a wooden boardwalk through the reeds, which describes a loop and rejoins the main path further along. If you use the bird hides, you have the best chance of observing the waterfowl on the pool. Mallard and moorhen are common, with heron, redshank and water rail seen on occasion. The reeds also attract a variety of warblers, and flycatchers are sometimes present in some number. Willowy areas are more often favoured by

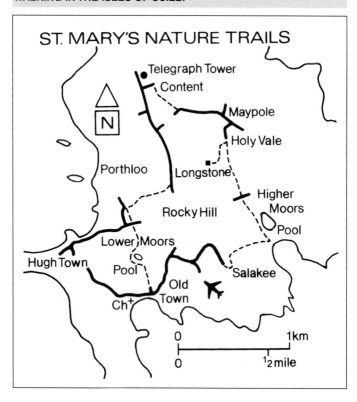

ST. MARY'S NATURE TRAILS

thrushes and blackbirds. The wetlands are covered in reeds, rushes and sedges, with interesting orchids, irises and other flowers that favour wet ground.

A gate at the end of the path leads onto a road. Cross over the road and go through another gate to continue. A short stretch of the nature trail weaves through a flowery field to pass through a gate onto another road. Turn right along a dirt road that is flanked by trees as it rises. You reach a junction with another road at Farmer Brown's Bulb Shop. Turn left and follow this road gently uphill, keeping an eye peeled for kestrels searching for small prey in the surrounding fields. Avoid other roads heading left and right, and aim for the cylindrical granite building called the Telegraph Tower. This stands on the highest point in the Isles of Scilly, amid houses and an array of communication masts, at a mere 166ft (51m).

Backtrack along the road a short way and turn left. The tarmac quickly gives way to a stony track, and you turn right to pass a farm at Content. Walk straight along the track to reach the next road, where you turn left to pass the Sage House Nursing and Residential Home. When a triangular road junction is reached at Maypole, keep right, then turn right down a narrower road. This leads into Holy Vale, where tradition asserts that there was once a convent or monk's cell. There are a few houses in the vale, surrounded by gardens of exotic vegetation.

There's a detour you could make at this point to include a visit to the Longstone Heritage Centre in the middle of St. Mary's. You'll see a couple of little notices giving route directions from Holy Vale, but basically you turn right at the bottom of the road, then left to pass houses and follow a narrow path along the edge of a woodland. When you reach a broader track, simply turn right and walk up to the Heritage Centre. There are plenty of old photographs and displays relating to the history and heritage of the Isles of Scilly, as well as a café, souvenir shop and putting green. After making a visit, retrace your steps faithfully to return to Holy Vale and continue the walk.

The road in Holy Vale gives way to a narrow path that runs through the Holy Vale Nature Reserve. Trees stand very close together on either side of the narrow path, and the roots can be slippery underfoot. The path is on an earthen embankment above a marsh, and the place seems like a jungle. It's one of the few places around the Isles of Scilly where you can walk among tall, densely planted trees. Emerging from the trees, cross a road and go through a gate to continue along the Higher Moors nature trail. The path is gritty underfoot as it passes through reedy and bushy areas, then there is a boardwalk section and two bird hides off to the left, overlooking a reedy pool. Again, it's worth taking a break to study the waterfowl, though sometimes the place is invaded by noisy black-headed gulls. When you go through a gate at the end of the path you are within a few paces of the shore at Porth Hellick, not far from a monument to Sir Cloudesley Shovell.

Swing round to the right after passing through the gate,

following a path through bracken away from the shore. The path goes through another gate and is flanked by hedgerows. Walk uphill to pass the buildings at Salakee, then turn left and right, then right again at a junction of paths to climb to a road alongside the little airport. Keep right as you follow the road around the perimeter of the airstrip, and take heed of the warning signs and pedestrian traffic lights that warn of aircraft taking off or landing. Follow the access road downhill from the airport and turn left at a junction with another road. This road leads past the Lock Stock & Barrel pub on its way back to Old Town.

Facilities on the nature trails

- Old Town has **food and drink** available at the Old Town Café and the Lock Stock & Barrel. The Longstone Heritage Centre has a café off-route above Holy Vale.
- Tolman House, The Withies and Blue Carn Cottage provide **accommodation** at Old Town. There is also **self-catering** accommodation available at Old Town and Telegraph.
- The airport **minibus** shuttle operates between the airport, Old Town and Hugh Town.

In addition, all the facilities of Hugh Town lie close to the nature trails.

WALK 5:

THE GUGH

Sometimes you can walk over to The Gugh (see map below), more simply referred to as Gugh, and sometimes you can't. It all depends on the state of the tides. A high tide covers a sand and shingle bar that links Gugh with St. Agnes, and the water in Porth Conger and The Cove merges to become a single channel. Although The Bar is out of water for more time than it's underwater, that's no consolation if you arrive just as it's being submerged. Tide tables are available from the Tourist Information Centre in Hugh Town. Gugh is the smallest of the inhabited Isles of Scilly, having only two households. It's a rugged little island, with so few people walking its paths that they are quite narrow in places. A circuit around the island takes only an hour or so, and if the bar is clear then you can easily combine a quick spin around Gugh with a walk around the entire coastline of St. Agnes.

The route

Distance: *2½ miles (4km)*
Start: *The Quay on St. Agnes, 884086*

It's fair to say that this walk should start at The Quay on St. Agnes, as there are no direct ferry services to The Gugh. Leave The Quay and follow the concrete road inland past a toilet block, passing the Turk's Head pub. Watch for a track leading downhill on the left, leading onto the shingle of The Bar and across to Gugh, but also watch the tide and be very wary if it is advancing while you are on the island. You see the two houses on the island clearly as they both face towards The Bar. Note the curious shapes of their roofs, which are intended to shed powerful gales in such an exposed location.

When you set foot on Gugh, turn left to walk clockwise around the island, taking in the northern end first. Either scramble on the rocks at the end of the point, or use a grassy path a short way inland

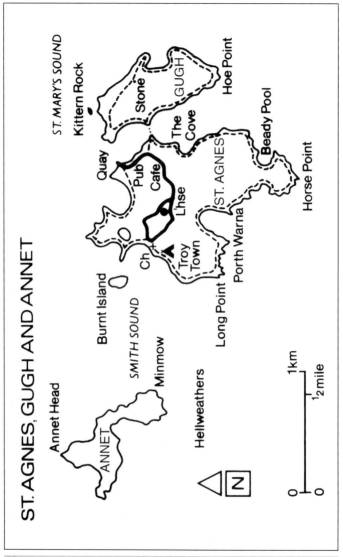

ST. AGNES, GUGH AND ANNET

The Old Man of Gugh is a Bronze Age standing stone with a distinct lean

to omit them. Kittern Rock is just offshore and looks impressive, and you gain quite a different view of it on the ferry to and from St. Agnes. Follow a path over the heathery crest of the island, called Kittern Hill, where you can enjoy the most extensive views from the island. Descend gently to a prominent standing stone known as the Old Man of Gugh. This is a Bronze Age ritual monument with a distinct lean to one side. Away to the west is a burial chamber known as Obadiah's Barrow, whose excavation yielded a crouching skeleton and a dozen cremation urns.

As you reach the rugged Dropnose Porth, you have two options. One is to cut inland across the island and return directly to The Bar. The other is to continue around the coast and pass Dropnose Point. If you pass Dropnose Point, then you can follow a path across a grassy, bouldery slope and pass Hoe Point. After turning the point you walk alongside The Cove, with a view back to St. Agnes. When you reach The Bar you cross over and either turn right to return to the Turk's Head and The Quay, or turn left to explore other parts of St. Agnes. To continue walking around the coastline of St. Agnes refer to Walk 6.

Facilities on The Gugh

- **None**: no ferry, no toilets, no accommodation, and no shops, food or drink. Bear this in mind before you depart, and if you get stranded there by an incoming tide!

WALK 6:

ST. AGNES

St. Agnes looks deceptively small on the map (see Walk 5), but its coastline is heavily indented and the whole island seems to be surrounded by rugged tors of granite. The beaches are often rough and cobbly, but there are a couple of small sandy coves. With a favourable tide, you could combine a walk around St. Agnes with a shorter walk around the neighbouring island of The Gugh (see Walk 5). The two islands are connected by The Bar, which is a ridge of sand and shingle.

There are some curious features around St. Agnes, such as the natural granite sculpture called the Nag's Head, the cobbly spiral of the Troy Town Maze, and a very prominent disused lighthouse dominating the island from a central position. Views on the western side of St. Agnes take in the little island bird sanctuary of Annet, and the awesome jagged Western Rocks that have wrecked many a ship. Further explorations in that direction are best accomplished on the occasional trips run by knowledgeable local boatmen. The tiny Burnt Island, however, can be visited when the tide exposes a rough and cobbly bar on the north-western side of St. Agnes.

The route

> *Distance: 4 miles (6.5km)*
> *Start: The Quay on St. Agnes, 884086*

Leave The Quay and follow the concrete road inland past a toilet block, passing the Turk's Head pub. Watch for a track running downhill on the left, leading onto the shingle of The Bar and across to Gugh. If the tides are favourable, you could cross over to Gugh and walk round the island. Refer to Walk 5 for a detailed route description. To continue walking around St. Agnes, however, turn right at The Bar, and follow a path through some trees above the shore. Drop down onto a sandy beach at Cove Vean, then continue

St. Agnes Lighthouse is disused, but it remains a prominent landmark

along a path through bracken and over rock outcrops to reach heathery, bouldery slopes around Wingletang Down. The cove called the Beady Pool earns its name from the little beads that can still be found there from a 17th-century wreck. The southernmost point of St. Agnes is turned at Horse Point.

Walk around the rough and bouldery coast, then wander round the little cove of Porth Askin. After passing a big granite tor, follow a well-trodden path around Porth Warna, crossing a few stiles. The cove is named after St. Warna, who arrived in a coracle from Ireland and is regarded as the patron saint of shipwrecks. After passing St. Warna's Well and turning round the head of the cove, keep an eye peeled to the right, and you can detour inland a short way to see the Nag's Head. This is a natural pillar of granite that just happens to have a strange protuberance shaped like a horse's head.

Continue along a rugged path around rocky headlands at Long Point. Tors of granite have long ridges extending into the sea. Views take in the Western Rocks, the Bishop Rock Lighthouse and Annet. The Western Rocks seem to fill the sea with jagged teeth ready to rip the keel from any vessel that dares sail through them. Annet is a long, low, uninhabited island, protected as a nature reserve for important colonies of sea birds. Note the Troy Town Maze, which is made of cobbles pressed into the short grass in the shape of a spiral. It dates from 1729 and was made by a lighthouse keeper, apparently based on an earlier design.

After walking round Carnew Point the tors are smaller and a cobbly path above the beach leads past the Troy Town Farm campsite to St. Agnes' Church. Note the long slipways here, which were formerly used for launching lifeboats. The infamous Western Rocks have wrecked hundreds of vessels, and for many years volunteers from St. Agnes were the only people capable of rescuing survivors in time. Most people are content to follow a dirt road onwards and return to The Quay, but you can explore another rugged stretch of low coastline.

If you continue along the coast, a cobbly tidal bar can be used, at low tide, to reach Burnt Island. An extensive pebbly seabed at Smith Sound is colonised by rare species of seaweed and supports rich marine animal communities. As you walk further around the northernmost point of St. Agnes, passing a pool where a variety of birds can be spotted, cobbly paths give way to more even walking surfaces. When you reach a track, turn left to follow it back to The Quay and the Turk's Head.

If you have the time and inclination to explore further, then follow the concrete road up to Higher Town, through the centre of the island, where you'll find interesting places offering food and drink, such as Covean Cottage and Rose Cottage, with their delightful tea gardens. There's also the Post Office & General Store at the top of the road in Middle Town. You can approach the stout, white, disused lighthouse on the highest part of the island. A blazing beacon was maintained here from 1680, continually improved through the centuries with the use of oil and electricity, until a revolving light shone out to sea. This was extinguished in 1911 in favour of the little Peninnis Lighthouse on St. Mary's.

Facilities on St. Agnes

- The Turk's Head serves **food and drink** near the Quay and provides **accommodation**. Covean Cottage and Rose Cottage serve coffee, teas and lunches at Higher Town. Covean Cottage also provides accommodation.

- There is also a bulb **shop** nearby selling bulbs and flowers. The Post Office & General Store sells provisions and souvenirs at Middle Town.

- **Accommodation** at Middle Town includes Downs Cottage, Coastguards and The Parsonage. Troy Town Farm campsite is at Lower Town, close to St. Agnes' (Church of England). There are several self-catering cottages and chalets on the island.

- **Toilets** are located beside The Quay.

- Apart from St. Mary's Boatmen's Association, **ferries** to and from St. Agnes are operated by St. Agnes Boating, telephone 01720-422704.

BOAT TRIP – ANNET and THE WESTERN ROCKS

Annet is uninhabited and access is restricted. Landings are not allowed from 15th March to 20th August, but there are occasional boat trips and 'Seabird Specials' that will bring you close to the island. There are some rugged cliffs along the eastern side of Annet that are populated by shags and cormorants, but the most interesting features are largely unseen. The island is covered with thrift and beneath it are hundreds of burrows excavated by shearwaters and puffins. It's only during the breeding season that puffins will come ashore, spending the rest of the year far out to sea, where they are seldom spotted by people. Shearwaters also spend the entire day far out at sea, coming ashore to their burrows only at nightfall, for fear of attack by gulls during daylight hours. Naturally, following each breeding season, Annet is covered with the rotting remains of chicks and some adult birds that fell victim to the gulls. If you do land on Annet early or late in the year, tread carefully for two reasons: so that you don't turn an ankle, and so that you don't destroy one of the precious nesting burrows.

Annet and neighbouring St. Agnes (see map, Walk 5) are as close as you can get to the vicious-looking Western Rocks unless you take a boat trip out to see them. Some of their names sound quite innocuous, such as Rosevear, Rosevean and Daisy, while others sound threatening, such as the Hellweathers. The most distant include the Crim Rocks, Crebinicks and, of course, the Bishop Rock with its slender granite pillar lighthouse. The first attempt to build a lighthouse on the rock, using cast iron, was unsuccessful, and the structure was torn from the rock during a gale in 1850. The granite pillar dates from 1858, but needed extra height and girth adding in 1887. The lighthouse builders lived in small huts on Rosevear, now in ruins, sailing to work whenever the weather would allow. Lighthouse keepers tended an oil lamp until the switch was made to electricity in 1973. The light has been automatic since 1992 and it is no longer serviced by boat, but by helicopters landing on the precarious helipad on top of the lantern. You'll discover that local

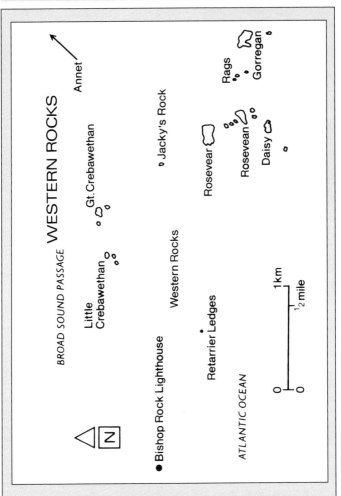

boatmen only take tours around the Western Rocks and Bishop Rock Lighthouse on the calmest days, pointing out shipwreck sites, grey seals and birds along the way.

WALK 7:

SAMSON

Samson is uninhabited and has no landing pier. It's also quite a popular destination and can sometimes be quite busy with explorers. There are only a few trodden paths, and anyone trying to make a complete coastal circuit will find that some parts are overgrown with bracken laced with brambles! However, there are enough paths to allow a decent exploration of the northern half of the island, as well as both the North Hill and South Hill. When you arrive on one of the launches, be sure to listen carefully when they announce their departure time. Landing is usually achieved by running the launch aground on the sandy Bar Point, with passengers having to 'walk the plank' pirate-style down onto the beach!

Samson is managed as a nature reserve by the Isles of Scilly Environmental Trust, which is keen to preserve its flora, fauna and archaeological remains. Neolithic pottery has been found. Bronze Age burial chambers and alignments of cairns date as far back as 4500 years. At low tide on the sandy Samson Flats you can distinguish ancient field systems – testimony to rising sea levels over the millennia. An early Christian chapel and burial site lies on the beach at East Porth. South Hill is divided into small fields by drystone walls, and a number of ruined farmsteads can be seen. In the 18th century the population was nearly fifty, but around 1855 the last elderly inhabitants were evacuated by Augustus Smith of Tresco, and the island has been uninhabited ever since. Smith tried to create a deer park on Samson, but it wasn't a success.

Invasive bracken covers former fields, but provides cover for woodsage and bluebells. Cushions of thrift grow on rocky parts of the island, and spiky marram grass covers the dunes. Heather covers most of North Hill. Colonies of lesser black-backed and herring gulls populate the slopes of South Hill. On the tidal flats

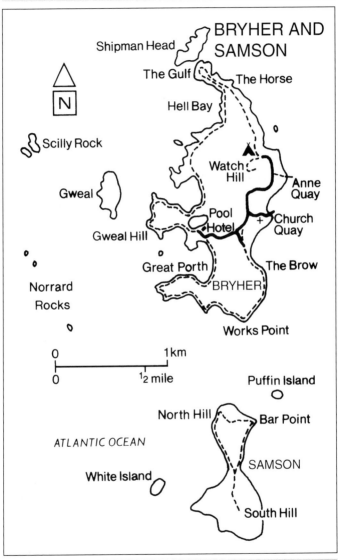

BRYHER AND
SAMSON

Shipman Head

The Gulf   The Horse

Hell Bay

N

Scilly Rock

Watch
Hill

Anne
Quay

Gweal

Pool
Hotel

Church
Quay

Gweal Hill

Great Porth   The Brow

Norrard
Rocks

BRYHER

Works Point

0   1km

0   ½ mile

Puffin Island

North Hill   Bar Point

ATLANTIC OCEAN

SAMSON

White Island

South Hill

The interior of one of the ruined cottages on Samson's South Hill

you may observe oystercatchers, dunlin, redshank and whimbrel. Ringed plover and grey plover are often present, along with curlew, turnstone and sanderling. Wrens can be spotted among the drystone walls, while rock pipits, stonechats, dunnocks, kittiwakes and terns can be seen from time to time. Kestrels will overfly Samson in search of prey, sometimes joined by the occasional merlin or peregrine.

The route

Distance: 1½ *miles (2.5km)*
Start: *Bar Point on Samson, 879133*

As you step ashore on Bar Point and walk up the sandy beach, drift to the left, and either walk along the beach for a while or come ashore and pick up a narrow coastal path. The path runs along the foot of North Hill to a grassy, sandy depression in the middle of the island, known as The Neck, between East Porth and West Porth. If you wanted to continue around the southern coast of Samson, then bear in mind that there is no real trodden path through the bracken and brambles, and the beaches are uncomfortably cobbly for walking. Oddly enough, it was the southern half of the island that was formerly divided into small fields and intensively cultivated in the 19th century.

From The Neck in the middle of Samson, a path can be followed up a slope of bracken onto the crest of South Hill. This path passes a couple of ruined houses, whose empty doorways and windows can be used to frame interesting views of Tresco and Bryher. Looking carefully at the ground, you can distinguish the shapes of ancient hut circles and burial chambers, while a rugged little scramble over blocks of granite leads to the top of South Hill, where you can view the whole of the island in one sweeping glance.

Follow the path back down through the bracken to The Neck, then drift to the left to pick up another coastal path beside West Porth, leading to Bollard Point. By swinging to the right and climbing uphill, you can reach the heathery top of North Hill. Take the time to inspect a number of small burial chambers around the summit, then walk down to Bar Point when you see your launch approaching. Be warned that when the tide is ebbing, the boatmen like everyone to get on board as quickly as possible to avoid being beached between tides.

Facilities on Samson

- **None**: no toilets, no accommodation, and no shops, food or drink.

- **Ferry** services are provided on an occasional basis by St. Mary's Boatmen's Association. Take careful note of the pick-up times to avoid being stranded on the island!

WALK 8:

BRYHER

The launches serving Bryher sometimes complete a circuit, landing at Samson and Tresco too, allowing you to enjoy a spot of island-hopping. Bryher looks small on the map (see Walk 7), but its heavily indented coastline offers a good day's walk. There are some amazingly rocky points, as well as fine views of the spiky Norrard Rocks off the western coast. Heavy seas occasionally pound Hell Bay when westerly gales are blowing. It may look as though you could walk from Hell Bay to Shipman Head, but the sea has carved a deep and narrow channel through the headland, effectively making Shipman Head into an island, and thus denying access to walkers. Although the population of Bryher is quite small, the island offers a good range of services including accommodation, food and drink.

A walk around the south-west of Bryher will bring you as close as you can normally get to the Norrard Rocks, unless you take one of the occasional boat trips out there (see 'Boat Trip – the Norrard Rocks'). The rocks have the appearance of a sunken mountain range, with only the peaks showing. The largest rocks are Mincarlo, Maiden Bower, Illiswilgig, Castle Bryher and Scilly Rock. Access to the Norrard Rocks is prohibited from 15th March to 20th August. Gweal is a small island separated from Bryher by the narrow channel of Gweal Neck, with access available any time you can reach it by boat.

The route

> *Distance:* 5½ *miles (9km)*
> *Start:* *Church Quay on Bryher, 882149*

The route is described from Church Quay, but depending on the state of the tides, your launch may well leave you at Anne Quay. Even if you do start at Church Quay, listen to any announcement

View from Shipman Head down to Tresco and Cromwell's Castle

the boatman might make, as you may need to be collected from Anne Quay later in the day. Church Quay is sometimes left high and dry above the water by the ebbing tide. Anne Quay was constructed with the help of Anneka Rice on the popular 'Challenge Anneka' series on BBC television. As you'd expect, Church Quay is close to a church, and you can take a peek inside All Saints Church as you follow a narrow dirt road inland and uphill.

Climb up to a crossroads and turn left over a rise. Walk downhill and turn left down a track, then turn left again along a concrete road to pass Veronica Farm. A coastal track is lined with agapanthus blooms in summer, while Hottentot figs swathe the ground around Green Bay. A coastal path passes banks of bracken and brambles around Samson Hill. As you turn around Works Point on the southern end of Bryher, there are views of Tresco, St. Mary's, Gugh, Samson, the Bishop Rock and Norrard Rocks. Continue walking around Stony Porth and enjoy the exceptionally rocky scenery around Droppy Nose Point. The sea beyond is filled with the Norrard Rocks.

Leaving Droppy Nose Point, follow a path over the crest of Heathy Hill and walk around the lovely curve of Great Porth, passing a rocky tor along the way. The Golden Eagle Gig Shed houses an art gallery, and there are houses and headlands nearby, as well as the Hell Bay Hotel. A large pool also catches the eye, and a path leads between the pool and Stinking Porth in the direction of Gweal Hill. You can either follow a rugged coastal path looking across a narrow channel to the little island of Gweal, or climb to the top of Gweal Hill to enjoy more wide-ranging views. The panorama takes in the northern end of Bryher, parts of Tresco, and the Day Mark on St. Martin's, followed by St. Mary's and the Garrison Wall, Samson and St. Agnes, Annet, the Bishop Rock Lighthouse and Norrard Rocks.

Follow a path away from Gweal Hill, through marram grass and bracken, around the cove of Popplestone Neck, then rise over the heathery slopes above the rocky coast of Hell Bay. The sea is often uneasy around Hell Bay, and the shape of the bay seems to make the waves pile up, so that they crash into the rocks and send spray spouting skywards. There are attractively rocky headlands ahead that may also be battered by heavy seas. Follow the path onwards, as if aiming for the most northerly point on the island at Shipman Head. However, you'll reach a rocky point where you'll see that a deep rocky channel separates Shipman Head from the rest of Bryher. The sheer-walled rocky chasm, known as The Gulf, has a boulder jammed in its throat and cannot be crossed safely by walkers.

Retrace your steps, then follow paths that drift to the left, continuing over Shipman Head Down. There are lovely views over the channel separating Bryher from Tresco, taking in Cromwell's Castle above the Tresco shore and King Charles' Castle on the heathery slopes above. You can visit both structures by following Walk 9. It's also possible to see the lighthouse on Round Island peeping over Castle Down on Tresco from time to time. Stay high on the heather moorland until overlooking some houses. Descend and keep to the right of the houses to pass through a field on a trodden path. There may be tents pitched here, as the field is used as a camp site.

When you reach a track, you could turn left to reach the Fraggle Rock Café and Bar. However, it's worth turning right up the track, then turning left along narrow paths to reach the top of Watch Hill. The ruins of an old watch-house remain on the hill, alongside a more modern water tank. A splendid panorama from the hill overlooks northern Bryher, northern Tresco, Round Island, St. Helen's and St. Martin's. You can also see the Great Pool in the middle of Tresco. St. Mary's and the Garrison Wall are in view, followed by Gugh, St. Agnes, Samson, southern Bryher, Annet, the Bishop Rock Lighthouse and Norrard Rocks. Retrace your steps down the hill and follow the track down to the Fraggle Rock Café & Bar.

Continue walking along the dirt road away from the café and bar, noting the left turn for the Bryher Stores & Post Office if you need any provisions. The dirt road gives way to a concrete road in places. If your launch is collecting you from Anne Quay, then turn off to the left to wait for it. If you need to return to the Church Quay, then follow the road uphill past a telephone box and the Vine Café. Walk down to a crossroad and turn left to walk back down past the church to reach Church Quay.

Facilities on Bryher

- Facilities (from the west to the east coast) include the Hell Bay Hotel, with Bank House also offering **accommodation** nearby.

- The Golden Eagle Gig Shed houses a **gallery** on the west side of the island too.

- The only **church** on the island is on the east coast, All Saints (Church of England), above Church Quay.

- **Toilets** are also located beside Church Quay.

- The Vine **Café** stands on the road between the two quays.

- Soleil d'Or and Chafford provide **accommodation** near Anne Quay, but there are also several self-catering cottages and chalets on the island.

- The Bryher Stores & Post Office, Fraggle Rock Café & Bar and the Camp Site lie at the end of the road above Anne Quay.

- Apart from St. Mary's Boatmen's Association, **ferries** to and from Bryher are operated by Bryher Boat Services, telephone 01720-422886.

BOAT TRIP – THE NORRARD ROCKS

The Norrard, or Northward Rocks (see map, Walk 7), lie scattered throughout the sea to the west of Bryher and Samson. You can view them easily enough from Gweal Hill on Bryher, where the little island of Gweal is also prominently in view. Landings on Gweal are possible any time of the year, but it isn't usual for any of the launches to land there. The Norrard Rocks are remarkably spiky in certain profiles and have the appearance of a sunken mountain range, with only the topmost peaks showing.

The Norrard Rocks are closed to visitors during the breeding season, from 15th March to 20th August, and in any case landings aren't normally made on any of them. The rocks include Mincarlo, Castle Bryher, Illiswilgig, Seal Rock, Maiden Bower, Black Rocks and Scilly Rock. Seals are often seen around the rocks, resting on low ledges, and puffins can be spotted in the early summer well away from disturbance. Tours around the Norrard Rocks include unusual views of Samson and Bryher, and will often include a landing on Bryher or Tresco.

WALK 9:

TRESCO

'Tropical Tresco' is a phrase you hear around the Isles of Scilly. It refers to the fact that all manner of tropical plants are grown at the Abbey Gardens, on a south-facing slope sheltered by windbreak trees and bushes. The name of Augustus Smith is forever associated with Tresco. He took over the lease of the island in 1834, and as Lord Protector of the islands he was responsible for great improvements, though not always with the full support of the islanders. He introduced compulsory schooling, the first in Britain, and there were fines for non-attendance. A monument to Augustus Smith can be visited on a hilltop near the Abbey Gardens.

Tresco is a fertile island, with regimented lines of tall, dark Monterey pines providing the tiny flower fields with shelter from the winds. There are sweeping sandy beaches around the southern coast, and surprisingly extensive moorlands in the north. Fortifications abound around the coast, with reminders of the 17th-century Civil War in the shape of King Charles' Castle and Cromwell's Castle. The Abbey House is one of the most substantial buildings in the Isles of Scilly, but it is not open to the public.

You'll need all day to walk around Tresco, and maybe a weekend if you want to make really detailed explorations of the coastline and still be able to have a good look round the Abbey Gardens. The ruin of a 12th-century Benedictine priory lies at the heart of the gardens. (See the separate description of the Abbey Gardens for details.) Tresco can be reached directly by helicopter from Penzance, cutting out the need to use St. Mary's as a stepping stone.

The route

Distance: 6 miles (10km)
Start: Carn Near Quay on Tresco, 893134

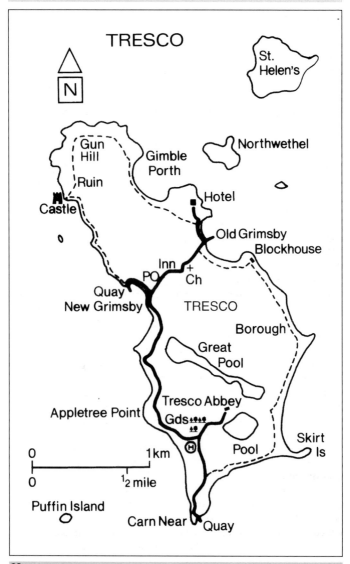

Launches to Tresco usually berth at the Carn Near Quay on the extreme southern point of the island. Some berth at New Grimsby, so check the landing and collection arrangements at the time you plan to visit. Sometimes the launches can be used to link Tresco and Bryher, without the need to return to St. Mary's. You also have the option of reaching Tresco by helicopter, landing at a small heliport near the Abbey Gardens. There is a transport service of a kind on the island too, in the shape of seating trailers towed by tractors along the narrow concrete roads.

Leave Carn Near Quay and follow a concrete road through the dunes and heath towards the Abbey Gardens. A little hill on the right bears the remains of Oliver's Battery – one of a handful of reminders of the Civil War. The road crosses a little heliport, where warning signs, lights and barriers alert you to incoming flights. Once you cross the heliport, the Abbey Gardens are to the right, but this walk makes a circuit of the island by turning left. Follow the concrete road, taking a right fork to avoid a stretch of road that has fallen into the sea. There are echiums and agapanthus growing in the sandy soil, as well as Hottentot figs creeping along the ground. Slopes of bracken and brambles give way to higher stands of pines. You can divert uphill to the right along a path flanked by rhododendrons to reach the Smith Monument, a slender pillar of granite boulders raised in memory of Augustus Smith. If you don't make the diversion, then keep following the concrete road onwards and enjoy the views across the channel to Bryher.

The road runs gently downhill and there is a glimpse to the right of the Great Pool in the middle of Tresco. Keep left at a junction beside the Estate Office and Post Office. As you approach New Grimsby, a right turn inland leads to the New Inn, and could also be used to short-cut across the island; otherwise keep straight on to reach the Quay Shop, café and toilets. There are occasional launches between the quay at New Grimsby and the neighbouring island of Bryher: easily the shortest ferry journey anywhere in the Isles of Scilly.

To the right of the quay follow a signpost for King Charles' and Cromwell's Castles. A narrow path runs through bracken and heather above a bouldery shore. It leads to Cromwell's Castle first, which is a cylindrical stone tower on a low rocky point. Steps allow you to reach the roof, and there are cannons aimed across the channel. A rugged path climbs up the heathery slope a short way inland to reach the ruins of King Charles' Castle. This hilltop fort was constructed in the middle of the 16th century to defend the narrow New Grimsby Channel between Tresco and Bryher. During the Civil War, a century later, it was captured by the Parliamentary army and partially demolished. Stones from the building were used to build Cromwell's Castle at the foot of the hill, in a much better position to defend the channel.

There are fine views around the northern end of Tresco from King Charles' Castle, taking in rocky Men-a-vaur, Round Island and its lighthouse, St. Helen's and maybe a distant glimpse of Land's End. St. Martin's leads the eye to the Eastern Isles, then the southern end of Tresco gives way to St. Mary's. Gugh and St. Agnes are followed by Samson and Bryher, with the distant Bishop Rock Lighthouse also in view.

Follow the heathery path northwards to Gun Hill, enjoying superb views back along the channel to St. Mary's, as well as across the channel to Shipman Head at the northern end of Bryher. Turn right and walk across the short heather using any narrow paths you can find. Disturbed ground along the way marks old, small-scale excavations for tin ore. Pass a couple of granite tors and rocky points as height is gradually lost. A coastal path leads through bracken around Gimble Porth, then a sandy path leads inland between fields. Turn left down a concrete road to pass some holiday chalets. Another left turn leads to the Island Hotel, if you fancy taking a break for food and drink in style. There is exotic vegetation around the hotel and lovely views from the outside terraces. If a break at the hotel isn't required, then turn right along the coastal road to reach the quay at Old Grimsby.

Turn right alongside some houses at Old Grimsby. You can go inland as far as the church if you want to visit it, otherwise turn left beforehand along another concrete road. A sign on the left points along a track for the Old Block House, which sits on a rocky outcrop on top of a low hill. A Royalist force was ousted from the Block House during the Civil War – the Parliamentary force arriving via the little island of Teän. The Block House overlooks the Island Hotel and the little islands of Northwethel, Men-a-vaur, St. Helen's and Teän. St. Martin's fills much of the view, leading the eye to the Eastern Isles and part of St. Mary's.

Cromwell's Castle on Tresco, built in the 17th century

Telegraph Tower is the highest point in the Isles of Scilly at 166ft (51m)

Bird hide overlooking a reedy pool on the Lower Moors nature trail

Troy Town Maze – a curious cobble circle made by a lighthouse keeper

A launch passes between the island of Gugh and a rock called The Cow

Cannons point across St. Mary's Sound from the Woolpack Battery

Walkers brave the storm as they pass Carn Morval Point on St. Mary's

A rugged tor on Bryher's coast, with some of the Norrard Rocks beyond

Palm trees and a view of the sea from Higher Town on St. Martin's

The Old Block House on Tresco saw action during the Civil War

Follow grassy paths away from the Old Block House, through the bracken and roughly parallel to the coast. You could drop down onto the sandy beaches either side of Lizard Point and continue to the promontory of Skirt Island. Note the tall, dark Monterey pines inland, and the tiny flower fields beyond them. Bracken gives way to marram grass and there may be agapanthus blooms in the dunes. As you follow the path parallel to the coast, there are views of the Abbey House away to the right. When you reach the concrete road at the southern end of the island, a left turn leads quickly to the Carn Near Quay. If you have plenty of time to spare, then you could turn right and follow the road back across the heliport and explore the Abbey Gardens, but you really need at least a couple of hours to do justice to the place. Birdwatchers who find they have a bit of time to spare could check around the Abbey Pool, which attracts a variety of ducks, geese, swans and other waterfowl.

Facilities on Tresco

Most of Tresco's facilities are concentrated in the middle of the island, between New Grimsby and Old Grimsby.

- The Quay **Shop** and café is at New Grimsby, selling provisions and souvenirs. **Toilets** are alongside. The Post Office and Estate Office are nearby, with the New Inn **offering food, drink and accommodation** a short distance inland.

- St. Nicholas' **church** (Church of England) occupies a space amid fields in the middle of Tresco.

- Close to the little settlement of Old Grimsby is the Island Hotel, **offering food, drink and accommodation**.

- There are a couple of **self-catering cottages** and **timeshares** on the island, but no guest houses, bed and breakfast establishments or campsites.

- The **Abbey Gardens** are on the southern half of Tresco and incorporate the Garden Café. There are also **toilets** alongside.

- In addition to St. Mary's Boatmen's Association, Bryher Boat Services also operates **ferries** to and from Tresco (telephone 01720-422886).

- There is a direct **helicopter** service to and from Penzance operated by Scotia Helicopter Services.

WALK 10:

TRESCO ABBEY GARDENS

This isn't exactly a walking route, but the Abbey Gardens are quite extensive and you'll have to walk around them to appreciate them to the full. It's probably rather ambitious to try and combine a thorough exploration of the Abbey Gardens with a complete coastal walk around Tresco, but anyone staying on the island for a couple of days will doubtless find time to do both with ease. There is an abbey, or more correctly a priory, in the middle of the gardens, but

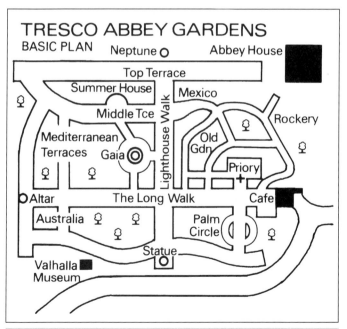

little remains apart from a couple of archways and low walls. This 12th-century structure was founded by Benedictine monks and was quickly brought under the control of Tavistock Abbey. Its ruinous state may have little to do with the 16th-century Dissolution of the Monasteries, as the site may have been abandoned long before that time. The priory site was used as a burial ground by the people of Tresco in the 17th century, until they acquired a cemetery alongside the new church of St. Nicholas.

The Abbey Gardens were planted by Augustus Smith from 1834. He not only collected plants himself, but also obtained specimens from Kew Gardens and encouraged seafarers to bring back flowers and shrubs from exotic climes. There are well-established trees from Australia, New Zealand, South America, South Africa and the Mediterranean. Arid areas have been created for cacti, while nearby terraces overflow with cascades of colourful flowers. Look out for ericas, proteas, lampranthus, cistus and many more. Most plants are labelled if you are puzzled by the bewildering number of species. The following route outline is only a suggestion, but it makes use of most of the paths and takes in all the varied areas of the gardens. There are around 3000 species of plants in the Abbey Gardens, which is bewildering even for a dedicated botanist!

The route

As you enter the Abbey Gardens there is a shop and ticket counter, toilets and the Garden Café. The old priory ruins lie to the right, in the oldest part of the gardens, but most visitors find themselves drawn along the Long Walk. Turning left at the end of the Long Walk leads you past 'Australia' to the Valhalla Museum. This is an interesting corner, where figureheads from shipwrecks have been restored and mounted around a courtyard. There are other items of archaeological or antiquarian interest scattered around, including cannons and signal guns. It's very much a hand-on type of museum, where you can touch and feel the exhibits.

Continuing along the path, which is lined with tree ferns, you intersect the Lighthouse Walk. You could follow this straight uphill, ending with flights of steps, to reach a statue of Father Neptune on the Top Terrace. Tall, dark Monterey pines provide a windbreak along the top edge of the gardens. If you turn left along the Top

Terrace, then left again, you can descend to the Middle Terrace. Here you have two options and, of course, both are recommended. You can explore the terraces of the Mediterranean garden and continue down to the Long Walk, then turn left and left again to reach the statue of Gaia. There's an exit back onto the Lighthouse Walk, which you can follow back up towards the steps.

Turning right away from the steps leads to 'Mexico' and a couple of arid areas such as the Pebble Garden and the West Rockery. You'll find narrow paths that lead you either down to the priory ruins or through the Pump Garden to reach the Long Walk again. If you cross the Long Walk you can follow another path to the Palm Circle, or simply retire to the Garden Café for something to eat or drink.

As there are literally dozens of species arranged in compact formations throughout the gardens, an attempt to list the species here is pointless. In broad terms you can expect to see palms of all types, acacias, eucalyptus, bananas, mimosa, aloes, yuccas, ice plants, cacti, honeysuckles, cinnamon, and flowers of every colour and scent. Exactly what you'll see depends on the season and on how much time you spend looking, as some species are shy and retiring, occupying little niches in rockeries. Colours change throughout the year as different species come into bloom – none more startlingly than the New Zealand flame trees. On hot summer days there are exhilarating scents carried on the breeze from a range of aromatic plants.

Facilities at the Abbey Gardens

- The Abbey Gardens incorporate the Valhalla **Museum**, the Garden **Café** and a well-stocked **shop** selling souvenirs and books aimed at gardeners and those with an interest in flowers. There are **toilets** alongside.

- The heliport beside the gardens, said to be the only garden heliport in the world, offers direct **flights** to and from Penzance, operated by Scotia Helicopter Services.

BOAT TRIP – ST. HELEN'S and TEÄN

It's thought that the little islands of St. Helen's and Teän were once joined to St. Martin's, maybe even as late as the 11th century. The water between the islands is quite shallow at low tide, but that's not to say you should chance wading across. St. Mary's Boatmen's Association runs occasional tours that sail around the small islands of St. Helen's and Teän, and landings are sometimes possible. The tours also include Round Island, but without landing there. Trips around these small islands will usually include a landing at Tresco or St. Martin's.

St. Helen's is a small and rugged hump between the northern ends of St. Martin's and Tresco. Its most notable feature is the remains of an early Christian church site, hermitage and burial place. The church, or oratory, dates from the 10th century, but there are earlier hut sites and cairns around the island. A ruined brick structure known as the Pest House was built in the 18th century. Any seafarers suffering from illnesses or fevers was likely to be put ashore there, where they would be unable to infect the rest of the ship's crew or the local island population. There is an interesting annual pilgrimage to St. Helen's on the Sunday closest to St. Ellid's Day, 8th August. Ellid lived on St. Helen's, and it was on this island that the Viking Olaf Trygvasson was converted to Christianity. He originally came to plunder the south-west of England and exacted a hefty tribute from the English King Aethelred the Unready. Olaf later became the King of Norway, and is remembered as one of three missionary kings along with Håkon the Good and Olaf the Stout. No doubt his experience on St. Helen's dictated the manner of his rule.

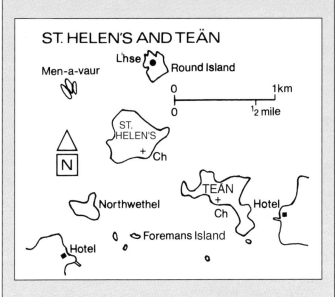

While landing on Teän is generally unrestricted, local boatmen have been observing a voluntary restriction between 15th March and 20th August. The beaches above the high water mark are used as nesting sites by ringed plover and terns, whose eggs are often indistinguishable from pebbles. There is a ruined early Christian chapel on the island. In 1684 a Falmouth family settled on Teän and the succeeding generations continued its occupation, along with occasional settlers from St. Martin's, but today the island is uninhabited.

WALK 11:

ST. MARTIN'S

St. Martin's has a dense arrangement of tiny flower fields on its southern slopes, and rather wild and uncultivated northern slopes. The two main settlements are Higher Town and Lower Town, and launches could use one or both quays when landing and collecting passengers. The walk around the island allows you to see at relatively close quarters how intensively cultivated the flower fields can be. There is a choice of paths on the northern side of the island, where you can either follow a narrow coastal path or switch to a broad, grassy path that slices through the bracken covering the higher parts of the island. The red and white Day Mark on St. Martin's Head is about as close as you can normally get to Land's End and mainland Britain while exploring the Isles of Scilly.

With favourable tides, your explorations of St. Martin's could also include White Island (pronounced 'wit'). This rugged little island is just north of St. Martin's and at low water a crossing can be made over the cobbly White Island Bar. The island has some impressive rocky headlands, and some parts are covered in deep, spongy cushions of thrift. There are also ancient field systems and cairns to inspect, as well as old kelp pits where seaweed was burnt to produce potash and other minerals. A thorough exploration of White Island would add another 1¼ miles (2km) to your walk around St. Martin's.

The route

Distance: 6 miles (10km) or (including White Island) 7¼ miles (12km)

Start: Higher Town Quay on St. Martin's, 931152

Although this walk starts at the Higher Town Quay, be sure to listen for any announcement the boatman makes: you might be collected from the Lower Town Quay later in the day, or vice-versa. Walk

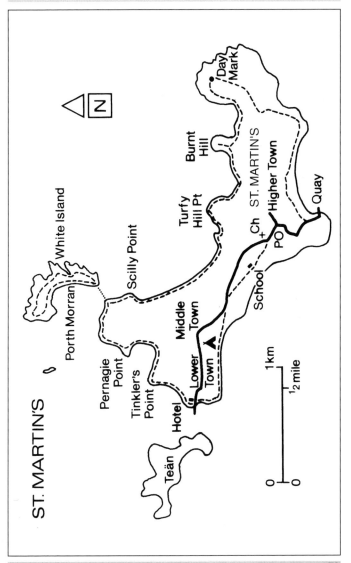

ST. MARTIN'S

Great Bay, Little Bay and While Island on St. Martin's

uphill on a winding concrete road, enjoying views down to the beach before turning left at a junction in Higher Town. You pass Web's Tearoom and the Post Office & General Stores. The road bends right to pass St. Martin's Church, but you should walk straight onwards beforehand, down a grassy, hedged track. When you reach a point where tracks cross, turn right to pass the white school building and rise gently to rejoin the road. Turn left, then left again down another grassy, sandy track. At the bottom you can either stay on dunes covered in marram grass or walk along the beach. Either way, just beyond a granite tor is the Lower Town Quay.

St. Martin's in the Isle Hotel at the Lower Town Quay incorporates the Round Island Bar and Teän Restaurant, named after the two little islands visible offshore. Teän is closest, while Round Island is easily identified because of its prominent lighthouse. The island tucked away behind Teän is St. Helen's. You can walk along a narrow path in front of the hotel, or a broader track behind, to continue around the coast to Tinkler's Point. As you walk round the bouldery Porth Seal you pass a water trough and a gate, then continue along a broad, grassy track with a view out to White Island. Note the spiral designs and other shapes that have been made by pressing beach cobbles and old ropes into the grass near the White Island Bar.

If the tide is out, you can cross the cobbly tidal bar and explore White Island, adding an extra 1¼ miles (2km) to your walk around St. Martin's. There are only vague paths around Porth Morran, passing old kelp pits and leading to an ancient cairn on the highest part of the island. As you return, it's worth seeing some of the rocky little headlands on the eastern side of the island. There is also an ancient field system on the narrowest and lowest part of the island. You can climb over the rugged little hill at the southern end of the island before walking back across the cobbly White Island Bar to return to St. Martin's.

A coastal path leads around the broad, sandy beaches of Little Bay and Great Bay. The path is narrow and runs through bracken or heather, laced with honeysuckle and other plants. If you find the path too narrow, then you can use other paths to move inland and follow a broad, grassy track along the crest of the higher downs. The lower coastal path runs above a rocky shore and turns around Turfy Hill Point. You could climb to the rocky little top of Burnt Hill beyond Bull's Porth or simply continue along the narrow path. There is a short, steep, rugged climb onto the heathery, rocky point of St. Martin's Head. The headland is crowned with a prominent red and white Day Mark and a ruined building. Although the Day Mark bears a date of 1637, it was actually constructed in 1683.

Views from the Day Mark stretch far across the sea to Land's End, with the Eastern Isles arranged in an attractive cluster closer to hand. Beyond St. Mary's is a distant view of the Bishop Rock Lighthouse. Samson and Tresco can be seen, along with Round Island and White Island. Follow a well-trodden path away from the Day Mark. Looking away to the left across Chapel Down you can spot what appears to be a standing stone on the heathery slopes. If you approach it, you might just be able to make out a carved face. The stone is thought to be an ancient statue-menhir, maybe as old as 3000 years, but it was only discovered and re-erected on this spot in 1989.

Follow the well-trodden path from the Day Mark to a triangular junction of tracks, then turn left and walk downhill. The track

St. Martin's Church at Higher Town on St. Martin's

becomes sandy and is flanked by tall hedges as it runs back to the Higher Town Quay. Along the way you pass signs announcing the Little Arthur Farm Trail, Little Arthur Café and St. Martin's Vineyard. These places are all open to the public if you follow the directions on the signs. Little Arthur Farm is run according to 'green' principles, while the vineyard is the only one to be established in the Isles of Scilly and is a developing concern. There are toilets and a sports pitch just before the Higher Town Quay is reached.

If you have to return to the Lower Town Quay for your return ferry, then you could either retrace your steps along the route you followed earlier in the day or follow the concrete road between Higher Town, Middle Town and Lower Town. The road passes most of the facilities on St. Martin's, except for those at the eastern end of the island.

Facilities on St. Martin's

There are three settlements on St. Martin's: Higher Town, Middle Town and Lower Town.

- Most of the island's facilities are at **Higher Town**. They include Web's Tearoom and the Polreath Guest House. The Post Office & General Stores, St. Martin's (Church of England) and Methodist Church are nearby, as well as the Glenmoor Gift Shop and North

Farm Gallery. Toilets are down beside the quay. St. Martin's Vineyard and the Little Arthur Café are out of the village.

- **Middle Town** has a gallery and the island's camp site is located in former flower fields nearby.

- **Lower Town** has St. Martin's in the Isle Hotel, which provides accommodation and incorporates the Round Island Bar and Teän Restaurant. The Sevenstones Inn is a little further inland. There are also a number of self-catering cottages and chalets on the island.

- In addition to St. Mary's Boatmen's Association, St. Martin's Boat Services runs **ferries** to and from St. Martin's (telephone 01720-422814).

BOAT TRIP – THE EASTERN ISLES

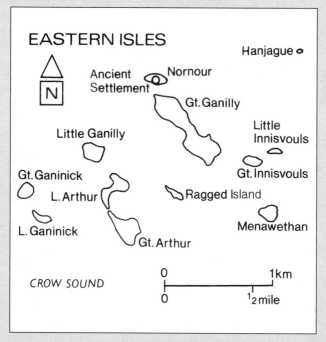

Boat trips often sail around the Eastern Isles, allowing close-up views of shags and cormorants on rocky ledges or feeding out at sea. The lower rocks are often used by seals, many of them reluctant to move until the rising tide lifts them from their resting places. The isolated rocky islet of Hanjague stands as a lonely Scilly sentinel, with the next landfall to the north-east being Land's End. Many of the boat trips that explore the Eastern Isles also include a landing on St. Martin's.

A launch passes a couple of the Eastern Isles heading for St. Mary's

Nornour was a largely unregarded island until a storm in 1962 suddenly unearthed a well-preserved ancient settlement site. Dating from the 1st century, the site yielded Roman coins and pottery, and the beach was strengthened against further erosion to preserve the interlinked dwellings. Interesting door jambs and hearth-stones are easily identified. The water between Nornour and Great Ganilly completely recedes at low tide, and when the village was inhabited the landmass may have been much larger. Occasional boat trips land on Nornour, while people with their own boats often choose to land on the larger islands of Great Ganilly, Great Arthur and Little Arthur too. Legend says that King Arthur was buried here after his final battle, again pointing to the existance of the lost land of Lyonesse. You don't have to believe in Lyonesse, but while you enjoy the peace and tranquillity of the Eastern Isles there's nothing to stop you dreaming about the place!

EXPLORE THE WORLD WITH A CICERONE GUIDE

Cicerone publishes over 280 guides for walking, trekking, climbing and exploring the UK, Europe and worldwide. Cicerone guides are available from outdoor shops, quality book stores and from the publisher.

Cicerone can be contacted on
Tel. 01539 562069
Fax: 01539 563417
www.cicerone.co.uk

OTHER COASTAL AND ISLAND GUIDES FROM CICERONE